DATE			

Reconciliation after Vietnam

Reconciliation after Vietnam

A Program of Relief for Vietnam Era Draft and Military Offenders

Lawrence M. Baskir & Willam A. Strauss

A Report of the Vietnam
Offender Study
Center for Civil Rights
University of Notre Dame

University of Notre Dame Press

Notre Dame & London

Library of Congress Cataloging in Publication Data

Baskir, Lawrence M
  Reconciliation after Vietnam.

  Includes bibliographical references.
  1. Amnesty—United States. 2. Vietnamese Conflict,
1961–1975—Draft resisters—United States. 3. Vietnamese
Conflict, 1961–1975—Desertions—United States.
I. Strauss, William A., joint author. II. Title.
DS559.8.A4B37   959.704'31   76-51245
ISBN 0-268-01597-X
ISBN 0-268-01598-8 pbk.

Manufactured in the United States of America

CONTENTS

FOREWORD

Throughout the Vietnam War, the saddest aspect of being president of a major university was having to watch thousands of young men undergo the anguish of making personal decisions about how they would respond to the war. Many sons of Notre Dame answered the call to arms, and some of their minds and bodies bear the scars of that terrible national disaster. There were others who accepted exile or stood trial to challenge what they thought was morally wrong.

I remember Dan's case especially well. Dan majored in theology at Notre Dame, and his draft board offered to exempt him as a conscientious objector because of his deeply held beliefs against war and human suffering. Dan wrestled with the prospect of being safe while others did the fighting. Unlike the millions who clung to deferments and exemptions, Dan could not accept his "CO" exemption. As a matter of principle, he stood trial and went to prison.

I remember cases of other young men, just as conscientious, who were fortunate enough to know people who could support their CO claims. I wrote on behalf of many of them and helped them gain their exemptions. But I always worried about the thousands of others—no less conscientious—whom I didn't know, and who for lack of an influential endorsement had their CO claims rejected. These worries shaped my views about amnesty because I thought that most draft resisters and deserters were people much like Dan.

During the past few years, I've spoken with hundreds of thoughtful men and women about the amnesty issue. Almost all shared my own misconceptions about bright, well-educated youngsters from good families or had a picture of radical exiles in Toronto, condemning American society from sanctuary. A few agreed with Nixon-administration spokesmen that people like Dan were "malingerers, opportunists, criminals, and cowards." These impressions have been hard to shake. With no hard facts and no objective analysis of the problem, it is understandable that so many of us have drawn the wrong conclusions from the sharp rhetoric of the amnesty issue and our limited personal contacts with these young people.

I accepted President Ford's invitation to be a member of his Clemency Board on behalf of young men like Dan, hoping to do what I could to make the president's program as decent and generous as possible. After I reviewed the first few dozen cases, the facts about draft resisters and deserters became clear. To my surprise, convicted draft resisters were often Jehovah's Witnesses, Muslims, clients of incompetent lawyers, and other victims of a fantastically uneven enforcement of the draft laws. Deserters were often youngsters whose low IQs or family problems had interfered with their soldiering and gotten them in trouble. In my mind, amnesty became more than a question of how to respond to people who had strong moral views against the war. It became a simple matter of equity and justice.

President Ford's clemency program was an honest effort to deal with the problems of these people. It did not help a great number of people, and some aspects of "clemency" were not especially generous. But it was an important first step toward a true solution. We have learned enough so that now we can debate amnesty the same way we debate energy, inflation, or aid to education—with facts, objective analysis, and realistic choices. Without President Ford's initiative, we would have nothing but our emotions.

When I left the Clemency Board, I wanted the American people to have the benefit of the experience I went through and to see the true dimensions of the amnesty issue. I asked two Clemency Board officials, Larry Baskir and Bill Strauss, to work full-time on the "Vietnam Offender Study" as faculty fellows of the University of Notre Dame, supported by a grant from the Ford Foundation. This report is a product of that study.

I hope that the findings and recommendations in this report can steer us all toward a practical, comprehensive resolution of one of the major tragedies of the Vietnam era.

Theodore M. Hesburgh, C.S.C.

PREFACE

In the fall of 1974, we were asked to take major roles in the implementation of President Ford's clemency program.* The amnesty issue had been debated for years, but until then we were no better informed about it than the average citizen. Then, as now, we respected the president's courage in launching his controversial program. The idea of "clemency" as a compromise solution struck us as reasonable, and we wanted to help assure that the president's program would be administered with fairness and compassion. We served on the staff of the Presidential Clemency Board for the year it existed, but we became increasingly concerned that the entire program, despite its initial promise, was a wholly inadequate response to the amnesty issue. At the same time, we recognized how many of our own preconceptions about Vietnam-era offenders had been wrong. We became convinced that something should be done to bring the American public to these same realizations.

Among those who shared our concerns was Father Theodore M. Hesburgh, president of the University of Notre Dame and member of the Presidential Clemency Board. He persuaded us to undertake a year-long study of Vietnam-era draft and military

---

*Lawrence M. Baskir served as general counsel and chief executive officer of the Presidential Clemency Board.

William A. Strauss served as director of planning, management, and evaluation for the Presidential Clemency Board, and director of the staff that prepared the Board's final report.

offenders under the auspices of the Notre Dame Center for
Civil Rights. The "Vietnam Offender Study" received support
from the Ford Foundation and began on December 1, 1975.
A special advisory committee was established, giving us the benefit of the experience and perspective of seven distinguished in-
divisuals who shared a keen interest in the subject.

As we began our research, we were surprised at how little
careful analysis had ever been given the amnesty issue. To gain
the necessary understanding of the problems of draft and military offenders, we had to engage in considerable research. We
assembled all available data relevant to the amnesty issue; we
went to nine military bases to learn more about their past and
pesent disciplinary problems; we interviewed over 100 counselors, lawyers, government officials, and affected individuals
throughout the United States; and we visited Canada and Sweden
to speak with the exiles. With the aid of several Notre Dame
law students, we researched the relevant draft and military law.
Through the excellent data processing facilities at the University,
we analyzed much of the raw data which emerged from the Ford
clemency program. Finally, we conducted a wide-ranging survey
of 1,586 men who were of draft age during the Vietnam War to
learn of their experiences with the draft and military.

The major product of the Vietnam Offender Study will be a
book, *Chance and Circumstance,* to be published in mid-1977
by Alfred A. Knopf and Co. The book will examine Vietnam-
era offenders in the context of how the war affected an entire
generation of Americans. A major part of the book will describe
the background, experiences, and present status of these individuals.

While we were doing research for the book, the American
public became engaged in an election-year debate about amnesty.
It became clear that important decisions about the scope and
context of any new program might be made shortly after the
1976 presidential election. Because much of the recent amnesty
debate has reflected the same confusion which has accompanied
the discussion throughout the past eight years, we believed that
there was a need for an analysis of the issues which could not
wait for the mid-1977 publication of *Chance and Circumstance.*
This report is our response.

The purpose of this report is to discuss the policy questions
that will inevitably arise should the president or Congress decide
to enact a new program. In the background discussion and the

description of our recommended program which follow, we have tried to provide the relevant factual material to allow objective, realistic policy judgments to be made.

It is important to recognize the limitations of government in dealing with a problem that has social, psychological, and emotional dimensions. Changes in official policy can provide significant legal and economic benefits, but they have a less direct impact on these other aspects which may ultimately be more important. "Reconciliation"—restoring a sense of national unity—can be achieved only if the public develops a more compassionate attitude toward the young men who paid legal penalties as a result of the war. Moral leadership from the president can help accomplish this.

The American people must show a new concern not just for Vietnam-era offenders, but for all men who were enmeshed in the conflict. Americans have largely forgotten the sacrifices of the millions of servicemen who served well in Vietnam, few of whom came home to the victory parades which greeted earlier generations of American soldiers. Thousands of combat veterans have struggled through years of unemployment and psychological turmoil. Hundreds of families still have no accounting for their missing sons, husbands, and fathers. All of these people deserve more understanding and official attention than they have received until now. This report addresses only the situation of Vietnam-era offenders, but any program for them should be part of a comprehensive national effort to address the needs and problems of all Americans who still bear the burdens of Vietnam.

"Amnesty" has always been a controversial term. For eight years, the amnesty issue has usually been framed in terms of the rightness or wrongness of the war. This framework has postponed an effective policy solution; it has also distorted the vocabulary. The words "amnesty," "clemency," and "pardon" have acquired a polemical quality, and their meanings vary according to one's own attitude about what should be done. The key issue is not whether we have "amnesty," "clemency," or "pardons," but what the program would do. In this report we have tried to use more neutral terminology leaving to others to decide what label, if any, should be chosen. We have also avoided such terms as "draft evader," "war resister," and "deserter," all of which have acquired controversial meanings which detract from an objective analysis of the problem. We prefer the more

neutral terms of "draft offender" and "military offender," by
which we mean nothing more than that an individual has been
or could still be punished for a violation of law. Our use of the
term implies no judgment on the individual's legal guilt or moral
culpability.

We must caution the reader not to interpret our statistics as
precise measures of the scope of the issue. Although we have
presented the best available amnesty data in this report, almost
none of the statistics can be established with certainty. What is
important is not a precise number or percentage, but its general
magnitude. We are confident that our data, a great deal of which
is new, is sufficiently accurate to put the amnesty issue in its
proper perspective. A more detailed description of the amnesty
data is presented in the appendix to this report.

We wish to thank the many people who have given their time,
energy, interest, and advice in the preparation of this report. We
are especially indebted to the members of our advisory committee, Hon. Charles McC. Mathias, Jr., Professor Morris Janowitz,
Professor Jefferson Fordham, William Klaus, Esq., Mr. Eddie
Williams, Mr. Roger Kelley, and the chairman, Father Hesburgh;
to Dr. Donald Kommers, director of the Civil Rights Center; to
Jim Carr, Rick Drucker, Barbara Gaal, Bonnie Katz, Tom Linn,
Bill Miller, Rob Quartel, Bill Valentine, Mike Wise, Susan Zwick,
and the many other fine people who helped immeasurably with
our research; to the Ford Foundation; and above all to our research assistant Larry Vogel, and our secretary Paddy Talboys
Shakin. Without everyone's help, this report would not have
been possible.

Lawrence M. Baskir
William A. Strauss
Faculty Fellows,
University of Notre Dame

SUMMARY

For over twelve years, America has been torn by the conflict
in Vietnam and its aftermath. Even now, two years after President
Ford's effort to "bind the nation's wounds" through a clemency
program, the amnesty debate remains divisive. Advocates see amnesty as a way to make Americans face the lessons of Vietnam.
Critics believe that it would be an insult to the veterans who served
honorably and an impediment to America's ability to fight future wars. The issue remains at an impasse.

This impasse will only be broken when the public gains a better understanding of the issue. Today, despite years of controversy, the American people know almost nothing about the young
men they label as "draft evaders" and "deserters." The media and
the public have always focused on those who were the most
visible—the politically active exiles in Canada. As a result, Americans have developed a number of distorted views about the subject. Consider the following:

Who would "amnesty" be for?

Myth: The purpose of "amnesty" would be to bring home as
       many as 100,000 "draft resisters" and "deserters" from
       Canada and Sweden.

   Fact: A half-million people could benefit from a new program,
           and many of them are not "draft evaders" or "deserters."

1

Only 10,000 are exiles in Canada or elsewhere, most of whom have permanently settled in their new countries.

Myth: "Draft evaders" and "deserters" were white, well educated, and staunchly antiwar.

Fact: The overwhelming majority of Vietnam-era offenders came from underprivileged backgrounds. Almost half of all "draft evaders" were members of minority groups who never registered for the draft. Three-quarters of the "deserters" were high-school dropouts, and less than 1 percent ever graduated from college. Most offenses were motivated primarily by personal or family problems.

What did "draft evaders" do?

Myth: Young men who avoided military service were punished.

Fact: Draft avoidance was widespread among the 27,000,000 men of draft age during the Vietnam era. Sixteen million never served in the military, two-thirds of whom took positive steps to avoid the draft through legal means. Just 8,800 were convicted for "draft evasion."

Myth: People who were punished as "draft evaders" did something worse than those who avoided the draft through legal means.

Fact: "Draft evaders" were far less manipulative and shrewd than millions of others who avoided the draft without penalty. Usually, "draft evaders" were unable or unwilling to take advantage of the hundreds of loopholes in the draft laws. About one-third qualified for exemptions or deferments, but turned them down as a matter of principle. Many were Jehovah's Witnesses, Muslims, or Quakers, whose religion barred them from cooperating with the draft system.

What did "deserters" do?

Myth: Many "deserters" were cowards who fled from combat, endangering their fellow troops.

Fact: Very few "desertion" offenses were connected with service in Vietnam. Just twenty-four servicemen were convicted of desertion to avoid hazardous duty in Vietnam. About 2,000 others were punished for less serious absence offenses in the combat zone and another 7,000 for refusing to report there—a small fraction of the 100,000 servicemen who bear the label of "deserter."

Myth: For every man who "deserted," another one had to fight in his place.

Fact: For every one of the 7,000 servicemen who fled when ordered to Vietnam, there were three who left from American duty stations after completing full tours in Vietnam. Many fought with distinction, only to "desert" when they failed to receive adequate postcombat rehabilitation. Twenty percent of all "deserters" served full Vietnam tours—twice the rate of Vietnam service for the draft-age generation.

What has been the government's policy toward these people?

Myth: "Draft evaders" were sternly prosecuted.

Fact: Selected Service referred 210,000 "draft evader" cases to the Justice Department—but only 4 percent were convicted, and only 1.5 percent were sent to prison. Over 100,000 had their charges dropped because of procedural errors committed by their draft boards. An estimated 360,000 others violated the law but were never caught.

Myth: The government still considers it important to prosecute "draft resisters" and "deserters" with the full force of the law.

Fact: The government has come to acknowledge that these people should not be prosecuted severely. Fugitive "deserters" are no longer being court-martialed and sent to military prison. Likewise, the Justice Department drops hundreds of draft cases each year, and less than 10 percent of those who are convicted are sent to prison. Some "draft evaders" have been sentenced to as little as one-day probation or a $5.00 fine.

What did President Ford's clemency program accomplish?

Myth: The Ford clemency program required people to earn
        their relief by performing alternative service.

  Fact: Twenty-thousand "draft evaders" and "deserters" re-
          ceived unconditional "amnesty" as a direct or indirect
          result of the Ford program. Most people who were
          known fugitives at the start of the Ford program had
          their charges permanently, unconditionally dropped.
          By contrast, just 2,500 people are earning clemency by
          doing alternative service.

Myth: The Ford Program settled the amnesty issue.

  Fact: At present, there are about 500,000 Vietnam-era offend-
          ers who still face the risk of prosecution, suffer a loss of
          civil rights from their criminal records, or bear the dis-
          abilities of bad military discharges.

The amnesty issue is most appropriately viewed as a question of
social justice, not antiwar ideology. The burdens of Vietnam were
very unevenly imposed. The economically and socially disadvantaged did most of the fighting. They also paid most of the penalties for not fighting.

Whether the war was right or wrong, America should seek reconciliation with everyone who was its victim—the dead, the missing,
the physically or psychologically wounded, the unemployed veteran
the fugitive or punished offenders, and all their families. No one
should be asked to pay any further price.

The Program in Brief

This report offers recommendations for a program of relief for
Vietnam-era draft and military offenders. In brief, the program
consists of the following:

(1) A task force, reporting directly to the president, would
plan and oversee the implementation of the entire program. Most
of the program would be implemented by executive order, and a

legislative package would be submitted to Congress to enable the program to offer the most appropriate measure of relief. There would be an active effort to enlist public support and understanding for the new program.

(2) Relief would be offered to people who committed draft offenses and other forms of nonviolent civil disobedience motivated by opposition to the war; 3,000 fugitive draft offenders would have their cases permanently dropped. Approximately 250,000 persons who never registered for the draft would never be prosecuted; 5,000 expatriates would be allowed to visit their families or restore their American citizenship; 8,800 convicted draft offenders would receive presidential pardons, and past records would be sealed.

(3) The program would encompass all offenses against military discipline, not just desertion. Three thousand fugitive military offenders would receive immediate discharges. Approximately 250,000 offenders with bad discharges would also be covered by the program. Relief would be offered to all qualifying offenders who were not convicted by court-martial, but some cases involving courts-martial would be reviewed individually. Individuals offered relief would receive a general discharge, with veterans' benefits accorded only to combat veterans and persons with service-connected injuries. Others with substantial military service would have their cases reviewed individually to determine whether they have earned veterans' benefits.

(4) No relief would be offered to anyone convicted of serious combat-related desertion offenses or serious felony crimes.

(5) No condition of alternative service would be required.

Recommendations

Eligibility

1. The program should encompass all qualifying civilian and military offenses occurring between August 4, 1964, and March 28, 1973. Offenses outside this designated period should be included if (1) they were committed by draftees or draft-induced enlistees subsequent to March 28, 1973; (2) they occurred in Southeast Asia; or (3) they were motivated by opposition to American policies in Southeast Asia.

The Vietnam Generation

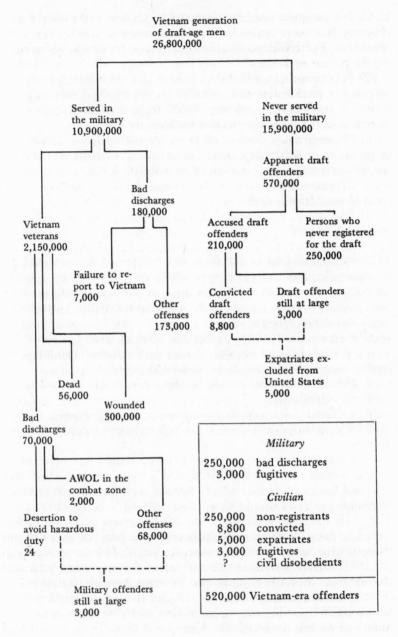

Vietnam generation
of draft-age men
26,800,000

Served in
the military
10,900,000

Never served
in the military
15,900,000

Apparent draft
offenders
570,000

Bad
discharges
180,000

Accused draft
offenders
210,000

Persons who
never registered
for the draft
250,000

Vietnam
veterans
2,150,000

Failure to re-
port to Vietnam
7,000

Convicted
draft
offenders
8,800

Draft offenders
still at large
3,000

Other
offenses
173,000

Expatriates ex-
cluded from
United States
5,000

Dead
56,000

Wounded
300,000

Bad
discharges
70,000

AWOL in the
combat zone
2,000

Desertion to
avoid hazardous
duty
24

Other
offenses
68,000

Military offenders
still at large
3,000

Military

250,000	bad discharges
3,000	fugitives

Civilian

250,000	non-registrants
8,800	convicted
5,000	expatriates
3,000	fugitives
?	civil disobedients

520,000	Vietnam-era offenders

2. The program should encompass all civilian and military offenses which were nonviolent and reasonably related to the Vietnam War. For civilians, this includes such offenses as (1) failure to cooperate with the draft; (2) destruction of one's own draft card; (3) nonviolent civil disobedience; and (4) failure to pay taxes. For servicemen, this includes (1) absence offenses; (2) other offenses against military discipline; and (3) any offenses which resulted in administrative undesirable discharges.

3. No serviceman discharged by court-martial for a civilian-type crime or still facing general court-martial charges for a civilian-type crime should be eligible for relief.

4. No person convicted in any state, federal, or military court of a serious felony crime should be eligible for relief.

Nature of Relief

5. Pardons should be the form of relief issued to convicted civilian offenders and servicemen who were convicted by general or special courts-martial. The issuance of pardons should be accompanied by a clear presidential explanation of their intended legal and social effects.

6. Pardons are not the appropriate form of relief for those charged with, but not convicted of, a draft offense. Pending draft charges should simply be dismissed.

7. General discharges should be the form of relief issued to military offenders.

8. All former servicemen should retain the opportunity to apply for an honorable discharge through military discharge review boards.

9. Entitlement to full veterans' benefits should be extended only to former servicemen who served a Vietnam tour which did not end because of misconduct. Former servicemen with service-connected injuries should be granted medical benefits only.

10. The Veterans Administration should review applications for veterans' benefits from individuals with two years or more of military service, under standards specially established for this program.

11. All former servicemen should retain the opportunity to apply for veterans' benefits through the Veterans Administration.

12. General discharges should be issued to replace existing discharges and must include no indication that they were issued pursuant to this program. The Veterans Administration must have

an independent means of determining whether a general discharge was issued pursuant to this program in order to establish entitlements to veterans' benefits.

13. Arrest records of unconvicted civilians should be destroyed. Records of civilian indictments and convictions and military court-martial convictions should be sealed, with use carefully restricted to designated purposes. Individuals should not be required to reveal the existence of these records. (This requires new legislation.)

14. Changes in official records should be made at the government's own initiative. Individuals should be personally notified about the changes in their status. These efforts should be supplemented by public information campaigns.

Conditions

15. Participation in the program should not require individual application except for (1) persons whose offenses occurred outside the designated 1964–73 period; (2) persons who were convicted of tax offenses motivated by opposition to the war; and (3) persons with two years or more of military service who seek veterans' benefits. All other eligible individuals would be identified through a search of appropriate government records.

16. No form of alternative service should be requied.

17. No oath or acknowledgment of allegiance should be imposed except for those seeking to restore American citizenship.

18. No test of conscience should be employed except to establish the eligibility of (1) persons whose offenses occurred outside the designated 1964–73 period; (2) persons convicted of nonviolent acts of civil disobedience motivated by opposition to the war; and (3) persons convicted of tax offenses motivated by opposition to the war.

Methods of Case Review

19. All individuals should be granted or denied relief according to designated categories, except a case-by-case process should be used (1) to determine eligibility in borderline cases; (2) to screen categories which include a substantial number of people who committed very serious offenses; and (3) to make veterans' benefits determinations for persons with two years or more of military service.

20. Case-by-case procedures should ensure due process and fair treatment. The scope of review should be confined to facts relevant to the specific questions at hand.

Categories of Affected Individuals

21. All charges against fugitive draft offenders should be dismissed. No pardons are necessary.

22. American expatriates and other foreign citizens who left the United States to avoid military service should be permitted to visit the United States.

23. Individuals who lost American citizenship because of the Vietnam War should be able to restore their rights by taking the standard oath of citizenship. (This requires new legislation.)

24. Nonregistration cases should no longer be prosecuted.

25. Individuals convicted of draft offenses should be issued pardons.

26. Individuals convicted of destroying their draft cards should be issued pardons.

27. Individuals convicted of federal offenses for acts of civil disobedience related to the Vietnam War should be issued pardons if their offenses were (1) nonviolent, and (2) motivated by opposition to the Vietnam War.

28. Individuals convicted of federal tax offenses should be issued pardons if their offenses were motivated by opposition to the Vietnam War.

29. State and local governments should be encouraged to offer relief to individuals convicted of nonviolent offenses motivated by opposition to the Vietnam War.

30. Individuals applying for federal employment should not be required to list convictions for nonviolent state and local offenses motivated by opposition to the Vietnam War.

31. Fugitive military offenders should be issued general discharges *in absentia* except for those charged with civilian-type offenses which warrant trial by general court-martial.

32. Individuals discharged for absence offenses should be treated as follows: (1) individuals with undesirable discharges should be issued general discharges; (2) a case-by-case review should determine whether pardons and general discharges should be issued to individuals discharged by general court-martial; (3) a case-by-case review should determine whether pardons and

general discharges should be issued to individuals discharged by
special court-martial for (a) absence in Vietnam, (b) failure to
report to Vietnam, or (c) failure to return to Vietnam from
leave; (4) other individuals discharged by special court-martial
should be issued pardons and general discharges.

33. Individuals discharged for nonabsence offenses against
military discipline should be treated as follows: (1) individuals
with undesirable discharges should be issued general discharges;
(2) a case-by-case review should determine whether pardons and
general discharges should be issued to individuals discharged by
general court-martial; (3) a case-by-case review should determine whether pardons and general discharges should be issued
to individuals discharged by special court-martial for offenses
which (a) occurred in Vietnam, or (b) were occasioned by orders to report for Vietnam; (4) other individuals discharged by
special court-martial should be issued pardons and general discharges.

34. Individuals now holding general discharges should not be
extended relief under this program.

35. Applicants to the Ford clemency program who were
granted immediate clemency or offered conditional clemency
should automatically be given relief under the new program.
Those denied relief by the Ford program should be given relief
according to the standards of the new program.

Implementation

36. The program should be a presidential initiative.

37. A legislative proposal should be submitted to Congress,
requesting (1) authorization and appropriations for the program;
(2) authority to grant general discharges with special limitations
respecting veterans' benefits; (3) provisions for the sealing of
records held by the federal judiciary, state and local governments, and the private sector; and (4) special exceptions to the
immigration law enabling expatriates to restore their American
citizenship.

38. A task force reporting directly to the president should
be established to plan and oversee the implementation of the
program.

39. An advisory committee, consisting of representatives from
the Defense Department, Justice Department, and Veterans

Administration should be established to assist the presidential task force.

40. The presidential task force should issue a public report at the close of its operations, offering such recommendations with respect to the draft and military discipline as it deems advisable.

41. The president should take an active public role in the program.

1.The Vietnam-Era Offender

As Americans have tried to cope with the experience of Vietnam, the amnesty issue has been used by many to reinforce their personal and ideological views of the war. To some, amnesty is a way of vindicating the antiwar movement; to others, its denial gives meaning to the sacrifices of those who fought. For those who simply wish to forget about the war, it is a means of reuniting the country after a divisive, tumultuous decade. Yet each of these views treats amnesty as a symbol, overlooking the fact that Vietnam-era offenders are real people with real problems. Along the way, traditional American principles of justice and compassion have often been submerged.

Most people hold a well-fixed image of who draft and military offenders are, what they did, and why they did it. To Congresswoman Bella Abzug, they were "the finest, most conscientious, most creative young people." Charles Colson once called them "cowards" who were "victims of their own character deficiencies." To President Ford, they were "young Americans [who] should have the chance to contribute a share to the rebuilding of peace among ourselves." Although Abzug, Colson, and Ford —and the millions of others for whom they spoke—drew different conclusions from the facts, they shared a basic misconception about these individuals. The image was one of well-educated radicals, keenly antiwar and disaffected with the government of their country, but eager to come home and participate in a post-Vietnam reformation of American society.

This image arose because public attention was riveted on the exiles in Canada and Sweden, objects of extensive press coverage throughout the Vietnam War. Most of the 40,000 or so who took exile during the war years tried to avoid the spotlight and become successful citizens in their new countries. But those who were more politically minded used this attention as a means of expressing their opposition to the war. Over time, most of the exiles came home—typically, without ever going to prison—but the roughly 10,000 who are still in Canada and Sweden remain in the public eye, dominating the public's thinking about amnesty. Having spent six or eight years in exile, most of them are no longer footloose immigrants. Instead, they are confirmed American-Canadians or American-Swedes with new families, new careers, and new homes. They are now becoming established in their adopted countries. Few see any point in returning to their old homes, where many of their neighbors might consider them traitors. Except for an occasional Christmas visit to see their families, these exiles have little interest in being amnestied or pardoned, yet it is around them that most people have formed their opinions about amnesty.

The hidden victims of the Vietnam era, and the biggest potential beneficiaries of any program of relief, are the half-million draft and military offenders who are in the United States.

Draft Offenders

Since the nation needed only a small portion of its young men to fight the war, the draft was designed to "channel" millions to engage in approved draft-avoiding pursuits throughout most of the war. Deferments and exemptions favored the privileged who could afford lawyers, doctors, counselors, or the haven of a college campus. Vast numbers of draft-age men saw that the hazards of joining the army outweighed the hazards of doing everything imaginable to avoid it, and draft counselors helped them wage a war of attrition against the Selective Service System. Millions of young men accepted their obligation to serve, but for those who did not, avoiding the draft was a virtual certainty if they got the right advice at the right time. As a result, the burdens of Vietnam fell disproportionately on the undercounseled, the poor, and the less educated. They did the fighting and the dying and they suffered the punishment for not fighting.

Those who went to Canada were less fortunate than their peers who got sound legal advice. Had the exiles been more clever and manipulative, they could have joined the millions with deferments and exemptions. Instead, they often fled without looking for help. They believed that exile was the only alternative to the draft or jail.

They were wrong. For every draft offender who went to prison, almost 200 others went free. Over a half-million young men apparently committed draft violations and could have been sentenced to five years in prison. An estimated 250,000 people never registered for the draft, almost half of them members of minority groups. Another 110,000 burned their draft cards, refused induction, or committed other offenses, but they were never charged. Selective Service officials did refer 210,000 individuals to the Justice Department for possible draft prosecution. Yet only 25,000 were indicted, 10,000 tried, 8,800 convicted, and 3,275 imprisoned.

What happened to the others? Many were given one last chance to enter the service, and some did so. Others failed their physical exams and were usually not prosecuted. But over 100,000 had their cases dropped because of technical defenses which challenged the actions of their draft boards, or else they were acquitted by judges and juries increasingly tired of the war. Skilled attorneys could invariably beat draft charges or, at the very least, negotiate for probation or suspended sentences.

Of the few who were sent to prison,* many could have easily avoided any penalty but chose instead to bear witness against the war by submitting themselves to punishment. Some voluntarily relinquished deferments or exemptions to express their opposition to the draft and the war. Others insisted on challenging the legality of the Vietnam War rather than resorting to procedural arguments to escape conviction.

A great many were faced with the choice between abandoning their religious beliefs or going to jail. Jehovah's Witnesses were forbidden by their faith from accepting conscientious-objector status, but their draft boards denied them the ministerial exemptions they sought. Muslims were considered selec-

---

*The available evidence suggests that the total convicted draft-offender population can be broken down as follows: Jehovah's Witnesses—20 percent; other religious objectors—5 percent; nonreligious objectors denied CO status—10 percent; others opposed to the war—45 percent; those whose offenses did not reflect opposition to the war—20 percent.

tive objectors and could not qualify for conscientious-objector status because they acknowledged that they would willingly fight in a holy war declared by Allah.

Not all of the Vietnam-related federal prosecutions involved failure to cooperate with draft boards. Many prosecutions were for nonviolent acts of civil disobedience arising out of the anti-war protests. Thirty-three individuals were convicted for destroying their draft cards, the targets of a deliberate Justice Department policy of selective law enforcement designed to end a dramatic form of public protest in which tens of thousands participated. Most of the thirty-three were sentenced to long prison terms. Another ten individuals were convicted for their war-motivated refusal to pay federal taxes.

Military Offenders

In the minds of many, the Vietnam-era "deserter" was a coward who let others risk their lives in battle—or a war resister who refused to fight as a matter of principle. Both of these popular images apply to just a few of the 100,000 servicemen given bad discharges for absence offenses or the 150,000 discharged for other kinds of offenses. In the main, they were poorly educated teenagers from disadvantaged backgrounds who could not adjust to the rigorous demands of military life. Relatively few fled to avoid service in Vietnam, and an insignificant number—just two dozen—were convicted for desertion under combat conditions.

Over half of all absence offenders left because of pressing family or personal problems that had little to do with their attitude about the war or their fear of combat. Many were teenagers who had dropped out of school, confused about their future plans. They joined the army with the hope that it would give them the self-discipline and maturity they did not have. Often, they had been trouble in civilian life and continued that pattern of behavior in the service. When military life proved too difficult, they decided to leave. Others had difficulty coping with life away from home. Their marriages were breaking up, or their families had to go on welfare because of the extremely low Vietnam-era military pay scales. In about 85 percent of all cases, opposition to the war was not the primary reason for their offenses.*

_____
*Three government surveys have tried to measure the antiwar motivations of absence offenders. All found between 4 percent and 12 percent to have this characteristic. A fourth survey, conducted by a civilian counseling or-

Almost one-third of all military offenders were educationally disadvantaged,* many of whom were brought into the military through the "Project 100,000" and "New Standards" manpower programs. Instead of calling up the reserves or drafting college students—either of which would have involved immense political consequences—the government met its manpower needs during the Vietnam buildup by accepting hundreds of thousands of recruits whose limited mental abilities would have disqualified them before and after the Vietnam War. These special manpower programs were politically justified on Great Society grounds. Ostensibly, military service would instill these underprivileged teenagers with self-discipline, give them the education they missed, train them for jobs in the civilian economy, and have them emerge as useful and productive citizens. Instead, they often ended up in combat, learned no useful skills, and returned home scarred by their military experiences. The attrition rate and court-martial-conviction rate for marginally qualified servicemen were both twice the rate for all other servicemen. For about 75,000, this meant bad discharges—one more handicap imposed upon people who were already disadvantaged when they entered the service.

A surprising number of bad discharges—about 50,000—went to veterans who served full tours in Vietnam.** Typically, they committed offenses after returning to American military bases because they could not readjust to the back-home army of spit-shines and routine garrison duties. These soldiers were given bad discharges despite their good or often heroic service in the war zone. Many were adjudged misfits and issued bad discharges for medical, psychological, or morale problems which could have been solved through better leadership and more compassion.

The 50,000 offenders who served in Vietnam greatly outnumber the 12,000 who were punished for direct attempts to avoid Vietnam service. About 7,000 servicemen were given bad dis-

---

ganization, found about 30 percent of all absence offenders to have been antiwar. The circumstances of these surveys suggest that the first three undermeasured, and the fourth overmeasured, the extent of antiwar motivation.

*These soldiers were tested as category IV and V of the Armed Forces Qualification Test (AFQT), placing them in the bottom 30 percentiles of intelligence.

**Three government surveys of absence offenders have indicated that between 18 and 27 percent served in Vietnam, almost all serving full tours. Data is unavailable for other kinds of offenders, so this 50,000 figure is an extrapolation of these survey findings.

charges for refusing to go to Vietnam, another 2,000 for absence offenses in the combat zone, and 3,000 for other Vietnam-related absence offenses; just 35 were court-martialed for desertion to avoid hazardous duty, 24 of whom were convicted of that charge. Several received very long prison sentences commensurate with the seriousness of their offenses. But the bad discharges they received were indistinguishable from those given almost 250,000 others whose misconduct was much less grave.

The military's response to disciplinary problems reflected the unusual stress it endured throughout the war. Because of expanding manpower needs, the army increasingly had to rely on young and inexperienced leadership at company and platoon levels. The young soldiers they had to lead displayed the same antipathy toward authority common to their generation. Other problems from civilian life became part of the military environment. Racial tensions mounted when black and white youths found themselves in circumstances of intense personal pressure. The drug culture invaded the military, fueled by the availability of cheap heroin in Vietnam. Flagging public confidence in the war weighed heavily upon all soldiers regardless of their personal views and rank. With no victory parades for returning soldiers, with confusion about the military mission, the will to perform was often lost. Vietnam-era military offenders were the double-victims of a service-wide crisis of morale. That crisis often influenced their behavior—and their punishment reflected the military's effort to maintain a disciplined fighting force despite these problems.

Early in the war, unauthorized absence and other disciplinary offenses were very frequently punished by court-martial. A conviction usually meant several months in prison and a bad-conduct or dishonorable discharge. Soldiers who committed lesser offenses were given undesirable discharges by administrative boards without standing trial. By the early 1970s, court-martial calendars had substantial backlogs of long-term AWOL cases. At the same time, Congress ordered the armed forces to reduce their active-duty personnel. Commanding officers responded by discharging servicemen who were disciplinary problems as quickly as they could. They offered these soldiers plea-bargans—fast undesirable discharges "for the good of the service" as alternatives to trial and possible prison.* These troops wanted out as much as the

---

*The number of undesirable discharges "for the good of the service" rose from 1,428 in 1969 to 29,618 in 1972.

military wanted them out, but many of them were only faintly aware of the hardship which those bad discharges would cause them later.

Almost all former servicemen with undesirable, bad-conduct or dishonorable discharges are denied veterans' benefits, including medical benefits for injuries suffered in Vietnam. They—like 300,000 others with general discharges—are handicapped in civilian life. The military claims the right, like any employer, to characterize the quality of a man's service—yet it has the power, unlike any other employer, to make its verdict stick for life. That verdict carries a stigma like that of a criminal conviction, making it hard for a person to find a job.*

Many Americans still fear that any relief for Vietnam-era offenders would detract from the sacrifices of those who served in Vietnam. But the public does not realize how many of the bad discharges went to veterans who fought in Vietnam. Likewise, many people forget that draft and military offenders were not the only ones who failed to carry out their share of the burden of the war. Over 90 percent of the 27 million men of draft-eligible age never went to Vietnam—and 60 percent never served in the military. Of the 16 million who never served, about half apparently escaped because of their deliberate, albeit legal, efforts to avoid the draft.** The public misconceptions about offenders have obscured the implications of the evasive action which the law encouraged and society condoned throughout the Vietnam War.

---

*Government and private surveys have consistently shown that 40 percent of all employers discriminate against former servicemen with general discharges and 60 to 70 percent against those with worse discharges.

**The Vietnam Generation Survey discovered that about three-quarters of its draft-age male respondents consciously tried to avoid the Vietnam War, either by manipulating their draft status, or by negotiating safe military assignments. Of those who never served in the military, 55 percent believed that "something I did" may have made the difference. Of those who did serve but never went to Vietnam, 42 percent felt that "something I did" may have kept them out of the war. This survey was based on a spot sample of 1,586 individuals in three locations, so its findings are not necessarily representative of the entire generation.

2.The Amnesty Issue

Four years after the last American troops left Vietnam, the American people remain divided about whether anything should be done for draft and military offenders. Dozens of proposals have been made and a presidential program has been completed, but the problem remains. The American people are still far from any consensus about what to do.

By contrast, Australia's experience suggests that the amnesty issue can be resolved and need not linger as a troubling carryover from the Vietnam War. In Australia, Vietnam was an issue just as controversial as it was in the United States. When Gough Whitlam of the Australian Labor party campaigned for prime minister in 1972, he promised to withdraw troops from Vietnam, end the draft, and declare an amnesty for all draft offenders and military absence offenders. Within ten days of his election, Whitlam accomplished all three of his campaign promises. He even allowed draftees to resign from military service, and three-quarters of them accepted that invitation. The Vietnam War—and the amnesty debate—quickly faded into Australian history.

America has not chosen to follow Australia's example, and our history offers little precedent for such a dramatic solution. Presidents have granted amnesties and pardons on numerous occasions, but never through programs which provide a model for a truly comprehensive post-Vietnam solution. George Washington's much-cited Whiskey Rebellion amnesty applied to a few Pennsylvania farmers. Abraham Lincoln was generous in forgiving Union Army

deserters but only if they returned to the front lines. Andrew Johnson tried to declare a full amnesty for southerners after the Civil
War, but he was hindered by Congress at every turn. It was not
until 1898, thirty-three years after the war was over, before all
civil rights were restored to southern leaders. Harry Truman's very
strict Amnesty Board after World War II denied relief in 90 percent of the 15,000 cases it reviewed, and pardons were only given
to draft offenders who had completed prison terms.

From a historical standpoint, the 1974 Ford clemency program
ranks among the most generous pardon or amnesty programs of
any American president. Still, the Ford program failed to resolve
the amnesty issue, and a half-million people could benefit from
relief.

The eight-year-old amnesty debate has always been enmeshed
in polemic and emotion. From the start, draft and military offenders have been identified with public acts of defiance against the
Vietnam War. In 1964 and 1965, hundreds of antiwar demonstra-
tors burned their draft cards in public ceremonies. In the years of
the Vietnam buildup, draft registrants refused induction at the
rate of over 20,000 per year.* Some took their battle to the
courts, but growing numbers fled to Canada or Mexico for sanctuary. By 1968, Vietnam troop strength exceeded half a million,
and desertion within the service became a serious problem. Four
servicemen from the warship *Intrepid* left their ship and conducted
a well-publicized journey from Japan to Sweden via the Soviet
Union. Suddenly, antiwar exiles began appearing all over Europe.
These exiles became a focal point for international criticism of
America's Vietnam policies.

From the first, the exiles were a foil for debating the merits of
the war. By 1969, some critics of Vietnam policy joined their de-
mand for an end to the war with the proposal that exiled draft
and military offenders be amnestied. The reason for such an amnesty, it was argued, was that no one should be punished for
standing up for what was right when the rest of the country was
wrong. Ironically, spokesmen for the exile community rejected

---

*Draft offenses were forwarded to the Justice Department at the rate
of about 30,000 per year, 75 percent of which involved refusal to obey
induction orders. Typically, no case was forwarded unless an individual
disobeyed three or four induction orders. A recent survey indicates that
as many as 5,000 people per year refused induction but never had their
cases referred to Federal prosecutors.

these early calls for amnesty; to them, amnesty was just a way for America to ease its conscience while ignoring the fundamental national flaws that had produced the war.

Eventually, however, the more radical exile groups began to embrace amnesty as an issue of solidarity. By 1972, almost all of the recent arrivals in Canada and Sweden were military offenders, many of whom had great difficulty finding jobs or adjusting to life in a new country. In a few closely watched cases, servicemen returned from Sweden to surrender to military authorities and were sentenced to long terms in prison. Many draft fugitives had little desire to return to America, but amnesty became a means of helping fellow exiles from disadvantaged backgrounds who were having serious difficulties as immigrants. At the same time, the American withdrawal from Vietnam made the amnesty issue the best device for exile groups to continue to remind the American people about the war.

Although the amnesty debate still focused almost exclusively on exiles, by the last years of the war the problem of Vietnam-era offenders had taken on new dimensions. Thousands of young men stood trial in American courtrooms, and many went to prison. As resistance to the war spread to ghettos and high schools, eighteen-year-olds increasingly failed to register for the draft, risking long prison terms if they were ever discovered. Tens of thousands of military offenders were given undesirable, bad-conduct, or dishonorable discharges for unauthorized absence, and large numbers of others were discharged for other breaches of military discipline. These draft and military offenders seldom formed their own pro-amnesty organizations and rarely viewed themselves as part of the public antiwar movement.

The early calls for amnesty culminated in the strong pro-amnesty stance of George McGovern as he began his 1972 presidential campaign. Amnesty quickly became a very difficult issue for him, and his position evolved toward the view of many moderates that a compromise solution had to be found.

The moderate position originated with Senator Robert Taft of Ohio, who suggested in 1971 that draft offenders be pardoned after completing three years of alternative service. He excluded military offenders, who were considered more culpable for having violated their oaths of duty. Taft's Senate bill

was followed a few weeks later by a similar House bill submitted by Congressman Edward Koch of New York. These
bills provided a foundation for the first public exploration of
the amnesty issue, which Senator Edward Kennedy of Massachusetts conducted as part of comprehensive hearings on Selective Service policies. During those hearings, the scope of the
issue was expanded to include military offenders, who were
pictured as would-be draft offenders whose opposition to the
war developed only after they joined the service.

Despite the rising interest in the subject, there was a consensus that amnesty was premature until all American troops
and prisoners of war had returned from Vietnam. When those
events occurred in 1973, amnesty was no longer an issue for
the indefinite future. In the twelve months following the
American troop withdrawal, ten bills and resolutions supporting some form of amnesty were introduced in the House of
Representatives. In May 1973, Congresswoman Bella Abzug
conducted an "ad hoc" hearing on unconditional amnesty; in
March 1974, the House Judiciary Subcommittee chaired by
Robert Kastenmeier, held the first formal hearings on legislative proposals for amnesty.

Testimony at these Congressional hearings was sharply
divided between advocates of universal, unconditional amnesty,
and those who insisted that nothing be done. The issue which
many had hoped would heal the divisions of the war instead
perpetuated the bitter feelings of the previous eight years.
Moderates of both parties who might have rallied to support
a compromise solution were reluctant to enter a debate which
still centered around the morality of the war.

With Congress stalemated, the only chance of an amnesty
solution lay with President Nixon. Despite occasional hints
that a conditional program might eventually be possible, he
and his spokesmen generally rejected any kind of amnesty.
Some of the strongest condemnations of Vietnam-era offenders
came from Spiro Agnew, Charles Colson, Patrick Buchanan, and
President Nixon himself.

In early August of 1974, barely a week after becoming president, Gerald Ford announced his intention to reunite the country by extending official forgiveness to Vietnam-era draft and
military offenders.* When the details were announced five

*See pages 27–48 for a description and an analysis of President Ford's
clemency program.

weeks later, the program drew much more criticism than the
White House expected. Antiwar circles criticized the Ford program as limited and punitive. They saw it as a cynical smoke-
screen to distract public attention from the Nixon pardon.
Conservatives regarded the clemency program as an insult to
the American serviceman, despite the requirement of alternative service and the limited benefits afforded by the program.
The most disappointing response came from political moderates. Despite its similarity to the Taft-Koch proposals of a few
years earlier, the Ford plan drew no public support from advocates of a compromise approach. They watched to see how
many would sign up for clemency, and when the disappointing results became known, they remained silent.

The Ford initiative quickly proved to be a political liability
for the administration. A low participation rate left the program defenseless against criticism from all sides. Long before
the program ended, Ford administration officials concluded
that it had been a political mistake to offer any kind of relief to war resisters.* Clemency Board Chairman Charles Goodell
labeled the program "a partial success at best," and President
Ford considered it "tragic" that so few people applied.

Despite this common judgment, the Ford program served to
mute debate about amnesty until 1976. Many people believed
that a fair offer had been extended and that despite its limited
results the amnesty issue was settled. The amnesty movement
had long been concerned that a half-hearted program would di-
minish the prospects for a comprehensive solution. With this in
mind, they vigorously opposed a 1975 bill sponsored by Senators
Jacob Javits of New York and Gaylord Nelson of Wisconsin to
expand and slightly liberalize President Ford's clemency concept.
On the other hand, unconditional amnesty bills submitted by
Congresswoman Bella Abzug of New York and Congressman
Robert Kastenmeier of Wisconsin fared no better than had similar bills before the Ford program. By the start of the 1976 presidential campaign, the amnesty movement was at a low ebb.

Amnesty rejoined the list of major issues after the announcement by Governor Carter that he favored blanket pardons for

---

*Curiously, a Gallup poll released in August 1975, toward the end of
the Ford clemency program, discovered a strong reservoir of support for
a compromise program. Eighteen percent of the public favored unconditional amnesty, 47 percent favored a Ford-style conditional clemency,
and 24 percent opposed any program.

draft offenders. He proposed a program that would be neutral in its judgment of war resisters' conduct, implying neither approval nor disapproval of their actions. Later, the 1976 Democratic platform expanded the Carter proposal to include military offenders, suggesting that their cases should be reviewed on an individual basis.

The Republican platform did not address amnesty, reflecting President Ford's view that there was nothing more to be said or done on the subject. The president believed that he had offered "a good opportunity" to earn a measure of relief, and he expressed no sympathy for those who failed to take advantage of his program. However, President Ford has not ruled out an extension or revision of his clemency concept. As he told a New Hampshire audience in February 1976: "What happens in the future, we" have to wait and see."

Despite the sharp differences of opinion expressed by vocal segments on both sides of the issue, it is clear that amnesty represents a major unresolved problem involving hundreds of thousands of Americans. As long as the controversy remains focused on a small number of politically active exiles, the impasse will probably continue.

3. The Ford Clemency Program

When Gerald Ford became president, amnesty was a hotly debated issue. Today, the debate has cooled, and more information is available upon which to base an effective national policy. As a first step to precede a final solution to the amnesty issue, President Ford's clemency program was useful. Without his program, the nation might still be as far from a solution as it was when he took office.

But standing alone as the single official policy of forgiveness, the Ford program was a clear disappointment. While there were some individuals for whom the program may have made a real difference, its overall effect was negligible. The basic offer of clemency has helped very few people. When the program is completed, the final tally will show that less than 9,000 people will have received clemency.* The real benefits of the program came through devices which were not explicit parts of the President's plan. In many respects, the Ford clemency program has the same unevenness and the same accidental quality as the draft and military justice systems which created the need for amnesty or clemency in the first place. Above all, it left the circumstances of hundreds of thousands of individuals unchanged.

*Over two-thirds of these individuals received immediate grants of clemency. By the time the final tally is known, perhaps 2,500 persons will have earned clemency by performing alternative service; another 10,800 will have dropped out of the program.

Facts and Figures

President Ford's clemency proclamation and executive order of September 16, 1974 covered four categories of persons: fugitive draft offenders; fugitive military absence offenders; convicted draft offenders; and former servicemen with bad discharges for unauthorized absence. To be eligible, an individual had to have committed a qualifying offense between August 4, 1964, and March 28, 1973. A total of 113,000 known individuals were covered by the program along with about 250,000 unidentifiable persons who had never registered for the draft.*

Several types of Vietnam-era offenders were excluded: about 150,000 former servicemen with bad discharges for nonabsence offenses against military discipline; those whose war-related offenses occurred before or after the designated period; and a far smaller number of draft card burners, antiwar protesters who violated any other federal laws, and aliens (including one-time American citizens who accepted Canadian or Swedish citizenship while in exile). Taken together, these categories encompassed perhaps 200,000 ineligible individuals.

Originally, the program's deadline was January 31, 1975, giving individuals four-and-one-half months to apply. By the end of December 1974, only about 3,000 had applied. In response to a late-starting publicity campaign, another 6,000 applied in the last three weeks of January. Responding to this increase, President Ford extended the deadline through February, and when another 7,000 applications came in, he extended it for one final month. Another 11,000 people applied in March, and the application rate was still rising when the clemency offer was terminated. About 500 applicants heard about the program after the deadline and had to be turned aside. Altogether, about 27,000 people applied, 21,800 of whom were later found eligible.**

The program encompassed four different categories of individuals, whose cases were reviewed by three separate government agencies. A fourth agency—Selective Service—monitored the alternative service performed by all four categories of individuals.

Fugitive draft offenders fell under the jurisdiction of the Justice

---

*See pages 80–82.
**Most of the others had general discharges, had been discharged for nonabsence offenses, or had committed offenses outside the designated 1964–73 period.

Department. Their cases were processed by the ninety-four U.S.
attorneys located throughout the country. Participants had to
appear in the district where their alleged offenses occurred. They
then negotiated agreements to perform up to twenty-four months
of alternative service, after which their draft charges were to be
permanently dropped. On January 24, 1975, four months after
the program began, the Justice Department published a list of
4,522 fugitives who still faced draft charges and were thereby
eligible for relief. Individuals who had previously been accused
of draft offenses were freed from all threat of prosecution if
they were not on the list. However, charges could still be
brought against an estimated 250,000 unidentified persons who
had never registered for the draft. Altogether, 736 draft fugitives
applied for clemency, and abot 500 were still enrolled in alternative service in late 1976. Those who dropped out can be prosecuted for their original draft offenses, and a small number have
in fact been convicted and sent to prison. However, many U.S.
attorneys are reluctant to prosecute clemency program dropouts.

Fugitive military absence offenders could report to any military base, from which they were sent to the Joint Clemency
Processing Center near Indianapolis. Once there, they received
immediate undesirable discharges and were offered the chance to
to earn clemency discharges by performing up to twenty-four
months of alternative service. The newly-created clemency discharge was considered to be under other-than-honorable conditions, without entitlement to veterans' benefits. However, about
sixty individuals with meritorious cases were given immediate honorable or general discharge which did make them eligible for benefits. The Defense Department announced that 10,115 fugitive
"deserters" were eligible, 5,615 of whom applied. A very small
number—perhaps 500—will complete alternative service.* The
Defense Department has suggested that those who fail to complete alternative service can be prosecuted for fraudulently obtaining a discharge, but no charges have been brought thus far.

Convicted draft offenders could apply by mail to the Presidential Clemency Board. Over 80 percent of those who applied
were given presidential pardons without having to do alternative
service. Most of the rest were asked to do three to six months of

*These were fugitives eligible for the program who had surrendered to
military authorities with the intention of participating. However, these
cases were not processed as part of the official clemency program.

work. One percent were denied pardons, usually because of serious criminal records. At the start of the clemency program, 104
draft offenders were still in prison. They were furloughed upon
condition that they apply for clemency; one individual refused
to do so and remained in prison. Some 8,800 individuals were
eligible, and 1,879 applied. About 350 were asked to do alternative service, and 100 are likely to comply. Altogether, 1,600
have received or will receive presidential pardons. The dropouts
and applicants denied clemency are under no legal jeopardy even
if they were among the 103 released from prison.

Former servicemen with bad discharges for absence offenses
could also apply by mail to the Presidential Clemency Board.
About one-third were given clemency discharges and presidential
pardons without having to do alternative service, and almost half
were asked to do three to six months of work. Seven percent
were denied relief, either because of serious criminal records or
because of aggravating circumstances surrounding their offenses.
At the start of the program, 170 court-martialed servicemen
were still in military prisons, all of whom were released upon
their application for clemency. Defense Department statistics
indicated that about 90,000 veterans were eligible, 13,585 of
whom applied.* About 6,600 were asked to do alternative service were asked to do alternative service, and about 1,500 are
likely to comply. Altogether, 6,200 have received or will receive clemency discharges and presidential pardons.** Program
dropouts and applicants denied clemency are under no legal
jeopardy even if they were among the 170 released from prison.

Every applicant asked to do alternative service had to contact
the Selective Service office nearest his home, which had to make
sure that his work met the standards set by the program. Of the
13,300 assigned to alternative service, only 8,400 initially reported. By late 1976, 1,500 had completed their service and less
than 2,000 others were still on their jobs. A total of 2,500 are
likely to complete their assignments and "earn" clemency.

Altogether, 113,000 individuals were eligible to apply:***

---

*This 90,000 number was an educated guess, based upon the Defense
Department's judgment about the proportion of Vietnam-era bad discharges which went to absence offenders.

**Another 1,200 cases remain unresolved, many of which still await
President Ford's decision. See page 39.

***Excluded from this figure and all percentages are the 250,000 non-
registrants, only 100 of whom (0.04 percent) applied for clemency.

21,800 (19 percent) applied, 20,800 (18 percent) were offered clemency, 13,900 (12 percent) received some measure of relief, and 8,800 (8 percent) are likely to receive the full benefits offered under the program.

At one time or another, close to 1,000 federal employees worked full-time on the program, the majority at the Clemency Board. Employees were detailed from other civil service or military jobs, so the visible cost to the government was small. However, the real cost of the entire clemency program was about $20 million or about $1,000 per applicant.*

The four federal agencies involved in administering the Ford program had very different experiences and problems. They must be considered separately to understand the strengths and the weaknesses of the entire program.

Defense Department Phase—Fugitive Military Offenders

The Defense Department did not share the President's personal desire to forgive military offenders, but it recognized that the program could serve an important internal purpose. By implementing its part of the Ford program, it could clear its rolls of as many fugitive cases as possible.

In the last few years of Vietnam War, each of the services adopted a general practice of discharging absentees administratively with undesirable discharges, instead of pursuing more time-consuming court-martial procedures. By 1974, the vast majority of absence offenders were being discharged by administrative procedures which had become increasingly streamlined. By the start of the Ford program, at least two army bases—Fort Dix and Fort Sill—were providing automatic undesirable discharges to returning fugitives.

The Defense Department clemency program incorporated this practice. Through special facilities, first at Camp Atterbury and later at Fort Harrison, it gave 5,555 servicemen immediate undesirable discharges, no different from what they would have received at Fort Dix or Fort Sill. In fact, many counselors in the United States and Canada encouraged fugitives to boycott the Ford program by going through regular channels to get

---

*The estimated cost of the program is broken down as follows: Clemency Board—$10 million; Selective Service—$6 million; Defense Department—$3 million; Justice Department—$1 million.

their discharges, and 846 people did so while the Ford program
was in operation.

During the six-and-one-half months of the Defense Department clemency program, the list of persons in deserter status
shrank from 10,115 to less than 4,000. This accomplishment
benefited not only the Defense Department but also the newly
discharged servicemen. Although they were given undesirable
discharges, they no longer had to fear being arrested, court-
martialed, and sent to military prison. Those who wanted to
stay in Canada or Sweden could now return to the United
States to visit friends and relatives whenever they wished. Had
this been the net effect of the clemency program, it would
have been of clear value. But by tying this streamlined discharge process to the "clemency" concept, the Defense Department program had some unfortunate consequences:

(1) As a condition of receiving an undesirable discharge under the clemency program, applicants had to sign an oath of
allegiance, reaffirming their loyalty to the United States. Many
did not mind signing this oath, and others simply found it an-
noying. But a real problem was faced by people who had made
permanent homes outside the country. Most had landed immigrant status and wanted eventually to become Canadian or
Swedish citizens, yet they needed a military discharge to regain the right to visit the United States. By declaring their
allegiance to the United States, they cast into doubt their allegiance to Canada or Sweden, jeopardizing their rights as immigrants. No oath was required for those who received administrative discharges through ordinary military procedures, so
Canadian immigration lawyers advised their clients to avoid
the clemency program and go to Fort Dix instead.

(2) The procedures at the Joint Clemency Processing Center
were exceedingly rapid. If an applicant arrived at 8 a.m., he
usually left at 5 p.m. with his undesirable discharge and alternative service assignment. Most returning fugitives were pleased
by this quick process, but many had cases warranting discharges under honorable conditions. They had been imporperly
inducted, wrongfully denied in-service conscientious-objector
status, wrongfully denied hardship discharges, or victimized by
other procedural irregularities. Many others had impressive
combat records, and their absences had resulted from postcombat readjustment problems. Through normal military channels,

these individuals would have had their cases carefully reviewed
and would have received honorable or general discharges. At
the Defense Department clemency program, they were told in
group counseling sessions that military attorneys would review
their cases with them for special consideration, but only if
they were willing to stay on the base for at least several days.
Most fugitives were pessimistic that this special consideration
would bring them anything better than an undesirable discharge.
Given their overriding desire to return home quickly, few tried
to get further advice from military or civilian counselors.

During the course of the clemency program, only about 100
individuals asked that they be considered for better than an
undesirable discharge. After a wait which often lasted several
weeks, about sixty ultimately received honorable or general
discharges with full entitlement to veterans' benefits. Military
attorneys who counseled clemency applicants believe that the
number of good discharges would have been in the hundreds
or even thousands if there had been time and staff to review
each case carefully. Altogether, barely 1 percent of the returning deserters received honorable or general discharges through
the clemency program—versus 10 percent of those who chose
to be discharged through normal channels at Fort Dix.

(3) The fact that returning fugitives received automatic undesirable discharges was quickly identified as a "loophole" in
the program. This "loophole" was not accidental. Senior Defense Department officials knew of its existence before the
program officially began. The alternative would have been to
postpone discharges until after completion of the assigned
period of service, but the military was eager to reduce its fugitive backlog as quickly as possible. A few days after the Ford
proclamation, spokesmen for the Defense Department admitted
publicly that there was no practical way to prosecute participants who refused to do alternative service. Responding to the
reaction of amnesty critics, the Defense Department shifted its
public position. Its General Counsel, Martin Hoffman, gave a
briefing at Fort Harrison in which he warned clemency applicants to do their alternative service or face possible prosecution for fraud. Technically, prosecution was possible, since
each person had to sign a promise to do alternative service
before he was discharged. But a prosecution could only suc-
ceed if the government proved that an individual had not

intended to do alternative service at the time he signed that
statement—an impossible requirement.

Clemency applicants who had the benefit of good civilian
counseling were not confused about the "loophole."* They
accepted their discharges without ever intending to do alternative service. Others had to rely on the advice of military attorneys in group counseling sessions, typically being told that anyone who dropped out of alternative service might be prosecuted.
This was enough to frighten some people into doing the work.
Those who boycotted the program and were discharged at Fort
Dix or Fort Sill faced no risk of prosecution.

The Defense Department clemency program would have been
of more benefit if it had dispensed with the meaningless clemency discharge, avoided deceiving people into doing alternative
service, and had simply been a nationwide expansion of the automatic discharge process at Fort Dix and Fort Sill. But despite
its defects, the program did contribute to an improvement in
the status of the fugitive population as a whole. The press covered it so thoroughly that thousands were encouraged to come
out of hiding or exile to apply. Without that publicity, most
might still be fugitives, fearful of arrest. Also, the Defense Department's tacit acceptance of the "loophole" led to a trans-
formation in disciplinary policies at all military bases. By mid-
1976, no returning absence offenders were being sent to military prison, regardless of their branch of service, the circumstances of their absence, or where they were processed.

Justice Department Clemency Phase—Fugitive Draft Offenders

Like the Defense Department, the Justice Department saw
the clemency program not as a way of extending official forgiveness but as a way of trimming its backlog of fugitive cases. Unlike
the military phase, however, its requirements for clemency were
strict and enforceable. Justice Department clemency required an
oath of allegiance, a waiver of certain legal rights, and eighteen
to twenty-four months of alternative service. There was a real
threat of prosecution for those who did not complete the program. Just 736 draft fugitives applied, a tiny fraction of the 4,522

*Without this "loophole," thousands more would have chosen Fort
Dix over the clemency program. As it was, many preferred the one-day
clemency process over the three-day Fort Dix process.

known offenders and roughly 250,000 persons who never registered for the draft. Five hundred were still enrolled in alternative service by late 1976. At least two of the 200 dropouts have been prosecuted, one of whom was sent to prison.

But despite its low turnout, the Justice Department cut its outstanding caseload to just 4,522 by granting a form of unconditional amnesty in perhaps 8,000 cases.* These actions reflected a tacit acknowledgment by the Justice Department that many draft cases had been pending so long that recent case law made them impossible to prosecute.

The first draft offender to surrender to a U.S. attorney did so amid fanfare and publicity in San Francisco, but it was quickly discovered that all charges against him had been dropped years ago. He went free—no oath of allegiance, no alternative service. Many others who surrendered to U.S. attorneys across the country were likewise told they had long ago had their cases dropped. Over the preceding six or seven years, the Justice Department had dismissed tens of thousands of draft cases, but U.S. attorneys and draft boards almost never informed the defendants. These men often wandered around the American antiwar undergrounds with assumed names or spent years in exile without realizing that they were free men. Thus it came as a surprise when the Justice Department released a preliminary list in late 1974 showing only 6,200 men still wanted for draft offenses.

Several weeks into the clemency program, a number of new indictments of persons not on this list were brought by a Boston grand jury, and concern spread that the Justice Department list was a trap for the unsuspecting. Senator Edward Kennedy of Massachusetts demanded a final, closed list of all persons still wanted for draft offenses. One month later, the department produced the "Kennedy list" with only 4,522 names on it. Except for unidentified nonregistrants, everyone else was free of prosecution, including the overwhelming majority of Canadian exiles.

Despite official assurances from Washington, some U.S. attorneys began to prosecute people who were not on the Kennedy list. Prosecutors complained to the Justice Department that they

*A survey conducted by civilian counselors indicates that about 17,500 people still believed themselves to be subject to prosecution when the program began. However, the department eventually listed only 4,522 active cases. Another 5,000 were excluded aliens because they had accepted Canadian citizenship (see pp. 78-80) leaving 8,000 who received "amnesty."

had submitted their lists without realizing they were final and binding. U.S. attorneys eventually produced over 800 cases which they claimed had been omitted by mistake. Efforts were made to have these names added, but Attorney General Edward Levi refused to prosecute these 800 cases, so all received unconditional amnesty.

Many of those on the Kennedy list, including some who applied for clemency, have tried to get their cases dropped in the courts. One Los Angeles attorney has represented hundreds of individuals whose names have been taken off the list. No official tally has been made, but reports from U.S. attorneys' offices indicate that perhaps 1,000 draft offenders whose names appeared on the once-final Kennedy list have had their cases dropped since the close of the clemency program.

Even those who have subsequently gone to trial have usually fared well with sentencing judges. Through Rule 20 of the Federal Rules of Criminal Procedure, those willing to plead guilty to federal charges could choose the judicial district where they would be adjudged and sentenced. Well-counseled draft offenders often negotiated for their cases to be heard in districts with reputations for lenient sentences. Of those convicted in 1975, only 9 percent have gone to prison, and many others were not even required to do alternative service as a condition of probation.

While amnesty was given those whose names wre kept off the Kennedy list, no clemency of any kind was offered to one very important category of draft offenders—those who had fled the country and accepted citizenship in Canada or elsewhere. About 5,000 exiles obtained Canadian citizenship in recent years. To qualify, they had to live as landed immigrants for five years and declare their allegiance to Canada. They were then considered "aliens" under American law. Even if they had not been charged with draft violations, they could not reenter the United States unless they could convince a hearing examiner that they had not left to avoid military service. The Justice Department enforced this exclusion through its Immigration and Naturalization Service, but it was the inaction of other Justice Department officials which led many of these exiles to give up their American citizenship in the first place. Had the U.S. attorneys informed them promptly that the prosecutions had been dropped, they would have been free to come home and might not have given up their citizenship.

The Ford clemency program did work to the advantage of many accused draft offenders. Without it, the Kennedy list might never have been published, and the legal status of thousands of fugitives might never have been clarified. For those not on the list, the program meant unconditional amnesty. Even for those who were on the list, the clemency program gave many of them the impetus they needed to find a lawyer who could get their cases dropped. Above all, every draft fugitive was able to get his legal status clarified for the first time in years. But the program did little to resolve the cases of those who still faced draft prosecution. Barely 15 percent of these individuals took advantage of the clemency offer, many of whom dropped out of the program. Only about 500 persons were still earning clemency according to the terms of the program as of late 1976.

Clemency Board Phase—Previously Punished Offenders

Composed of private citizens appointed specially for the task and ideologically balanced to reflect the full spectrum of public opinion, the Clemency Board symbolized President Ford's desire to "bind the nation's wounds" by finding a middle-ground solution to the amnesty issue. After some initial difficulty, the board developed a fragile consensus, and most board members had high expectations about what could be accomplished. But midway through the program, this consensus gave way to the same fundamental disagreements which have always plagued the amnesty debate. A minority of the board increasingly insisted that the president's concept of clemency should be narrowly construed. Because of the minority's influence in the Ford administration, the Board majority was unsuccessful in its efforts to modify the program. High expectations resulted in little more than recommendations which were rejected by other agencies and sometimes by the president himself.

The Clemency Board accomplished considerably less than the other agencies involved in the president's program. The Defense Department and Justice Department phases provided real benefits for people; through the "loophole" and Kennedy list, they unconditionally ended the fugitive status of thousands of Vietnam-era offenders. Through the Clemency Board's

activities, 273 people were let out of prison, and 1,600 convicted draft offenders received presidential pardons of uncertain meaning. But nothing of tangible value was done for the
board's other 14,000 applicants.

The nine oirginal members of the Clemency Board were
names on the same day that the President created his program.
None, including the board's chairman, former U.S. Senator
Charles Goodell, had participated in planning the design of
the overall program. From the start, their role was limited to
reviewing the cases of convicted draft offenders and discharged
military offenders and making recommendations about what
should be done with their cases. The board had no independent authority to implement any of its own recommendations.

When the board members began reviewing cases, they discovered how much their original impressions of Vietnam-era
offenders had been shaped by the rhetoric of the amnesty debate. In its first group of cases, the board tentatively voted to
send some people back to prison, deny pardons to 25 percent,
and require an average of eighteen months alternative service
from the rest. After becoming familiar with its cases, the
board sent no one back to prison, denied pardons to just 6
percent, recommended immediate pardons for 40 percent, and
required an average of only four months of alternative service
from the rest. They had expected to find intensely political,
well-educated, antiwar activists; instead, the typical cases involved highschool dropouts from low-income families whose
offenses were often the result of severe personal problems.
They had expected to find many acts of desertion under combat circumstances; instead, they encountered a great many returning Vietnam veterans who went AWOL only when they
did not receive postcombat medical or psychological counseling after completing their combat tours.

Many board members came to realize that the basic structure of the president's program was inadequately suited to
the needs of the people who were applying. The Clemency
Board had a number of ideas for making the program more
realistic and successful, but there was little that it could do
to change official policy. Instead, it could only make recommendations, usually with little effect:

(1) The low level of applications for the first few months
demonstrated that most eligible people did not realize they

could apply. The Clemency Board began an eleventh-hour public information campaign to inform the American public about the clemency program. In the four months before this campaign, the board received 850 applications; in the three weeks which followed the start of its publicity, it received over 4,000 more. Encouraged by these results, the board requested that the program be extended by six months to enable a more comprehensive campaign to be conducted. Instead, the president granted two one-month extensions and then ended the program.

(2) The board wanted applicants to receive something more than a mere certificate of clemency. The president's oirginal proclamation spoke only of "clemency," saying nothing of pardons or other forms of relief. Upon the board's recommendation, the president agreed to grant pardons to convicted draft and military offenders. But the board wanted these pardons to be reinforced by a presidential declaration relieving draft and military offenders of all future legal consequences of their offenses. The board proposed that federal agencies, and especially the Defense Department, "should disregard all pardoned offenses in any subsequent actions they take involving clemency recipients." A pardoned offender who had never done anything else wrong should be able to qualify for a better discharge upon application to the appropriate military discharge review board, or for veterans' benefits upon application to teh Veterans Administration. President Ford did not define his pardons, leaving each federal agency to make its own interpretation. All four discharge review boards and the Veterans Administration have taken the official position that they consider pardoned offenses to be sufficient grounds for denying discharge upgrades or veterans' benefits. Only the Civil Service Commission has interpreted a pardon to mean what the Clemency Board had in mind.

(3) The Clemency Board believed that the clemency discharge should be a meaningful improvement over the discharge it replaced. The Board wanted it to be a neutral discharge, neither under honorable conditions nor under other-than-honorable conditions. But the Defense Department resisted this suggestion and continued to designate clemency discharges as "under other-than-honorable conditions," making them virtually equivalent to the undesirable discharges which most military

offenders already had.* Rather than withdrawing the original
bad discharges, the department merely supplemented them with
notations about "clemency," contrary to the explicit provisions
of President Ford's executive order.

(4) The Clemency Board was determined to help former servicemen who had performed well in Vietnam before committing
their offenses. Over one-fourth of all Clemency Board applicants
were Vietnam veterans, some with serious injuries. Most had not
gone AWOL until after returning home. The psychological scars
of combat and severe personal problems drove many to leave
their posts rather than wait out the last few months before their
tours were up. Most board members objected to the military's
practice of discharging these Vietnam veterans with certificates
which denied them veterans' benefits, even medical benefits for
their combat wounds. The board recommended without success
that the president direct that these individuals be given veterans'
benefits.

(5) During its public-information campaign, the Clemency Board
sent letters to state and federal prisons throughout the country.
Prior studies had shown that many Vietnam-era veterans with bad
discharges were among the nation's 200,000 prison inmates, and
the board believed that the president's program could help them
find jobs after their release from prison. Over 1,000 inmates applied for clemency. Many had committed crimes so serious that
the board decided not to recommend them for clemency, but it
recommended that President Ford grant pardons to about 700
whose less-serious offenses were outweighed by other considera-
tions. Some were combat veterans whose civilian crimes resulted
from drug habits picked up in Vietnam. Others turned to crime
when their bad discharges kept them from getting jobs. These 700
case recommendations remained pending before the president in
late 1976, a year after the Clemency Board went out of business.

(6) Most Clemency Board applicants were asked to do three to
six months of alternative service. The board was concerned that
these relatively short assignments not interfere with fulltime jobs
or family life, so it asked Selective Service to make a series of
rule changes to make the alternative service requirement more
flexible. Selective Service implemented some of these recommen-

---

*However, a 1975 survey of employers found that the clemency dis-
charge was considered by them to be almost as good as a general discharge,
but veterans' counselors report that employers are not often looking upon
clemency discharges with favor.

dations, but not with the full measure of generosity which the board thought was necessary.*

The Clemency Board's disappointments cannot all be attributed to its inability to get its recommendations implemented. After the first few months, the board and its staff spent almost all of their time reviewing individual cases. Very little attention was given to the larger issues of the program. As a result, no one perceived many of the fundamental defects in the president's program. In particular, neither the board nor its staff fully understood the difficulties of trying to help undereducated, poorly counseled applicants. The only applicants most board or staff members ever met were the handful who took the trouble to appear personally at board hearings. They were articulate, highly motivated individuals who considered clemency or amnesty to be a very important personal matter.

The typical Clemency Board applicant was someone much different. He applied not knowing what he would get. By the time he heard from the board several months later, the clemency program had already passed out of his mind. He had never talked to a counselor, never corresponded with the Clemency Board, and had difficulty understanding what "pardon," "clemency discharge," and "alternative service" all meant. His attitude toward the clemency program increasingly became one of disinterest and confusion. Some of the 6,000 who received immediate presidential pardons never realized what they were or what they meant. Just 45 percnet of the people assigned to alternative service ever contacted Selective Service, and only 20 percent are likely to complete the program. The Clemency Board did not anticipate these problems and plainly overestimated its applicants' willingness or capacity to do even the shortest period of alternative service.

Instead, the Clemency Board offered its applicants benefits which few of them needed: pardons whose intended impact was never defined by the president, and clemency discharges which may be no better than the discharges they replaced. Perhaps because of these limited benefits, few people are completing

---

*For example, the Clemency Board recommended that all its applicants be given full credit for working fifteen hours per week on volunteer after-hours jobs. After a delay of several months, Selective Service agreed to allow part-time work, but it extended the option only to those assigned three to six months of alternative service, required them to work twenty hours per week, and made them double the total length of the assignment.

their three to six months of alternative service. In fact, those who drop out of the program may find that their involvement with the Clemency Board left them worse off than before. A senior military officer referred to them as "double deserters" who would have less chance than before of getting their bad discharges upgraded.

Selective Service Phase—Alternative Service

The alternative service phase of President Ford's program has been a major disappointment. Envisioned as a way to justify the program by having people earn clemency,* alternative service further reduced the already-low participation rate in the Ford program.

This aspect of the Ford program was destined for trouble from the start. Selective Service had been given this responsibility because of the agency's experience in monitoring the alternative service of conscientious objectors. This proved to be a fundamental mistake. The agency was extremely unsympathetic about extending official forgiveness to anyone who had committed draft or military offenses.

At the beginning of the program, Selective Service published alternative service rules which were so strict that few people could find acceptable work. To prevent jobs from being taken away from Vietnam veterans, for example, an individual could only fill a job for which there was no other qualified applicants. At the time, the nation was in the midst of a severe recession, and there were few employment opportunities which met all of Selective Service's standards. Compounding this problem, local organizations sometimes intervened to have clemency applicants fired from their alternative service jobs. For several months, Selective Service applied its rules stringently, terminating people who could not keep or find an acceptable job.

By mid-1975, the economy improved, and Selective Service began to ease its rules. The agency's budget was cut back sharply, leaving the clemency program as its major reason for existence. Agency officials then began to assume a more favorable attitude

---

*A 1975 survey of employers found that they looked upon pardons and clemency discharges more favorably if they were earned through alternative service than if they were received outright. However, only one employer in twenty-five applied this kind of distinction.

toward the president's program. Thousands of applicants had already been terminated or discouraged from staying with the program. The agency's staff had been trimmed so much that the personal job placement help which once might have been given clemency applicants was now no longer possible.

Only part of the poor alternative service performance is attributable to Selective Service. Much of the problem lay in the president's original concept of "clemency." Had the program been structured differently, it might have had fewer dropouts. There are three ways in which the program's basic design contributed to the failure of alternative service:

(1) Many applicants to the Ford program lost interest in doing alternative service when they learned how meager the benefits would be. Former servicemen stood only to receive clemency discharges—no discharges under honorable conditions and no veterans' benefits. Clemency Board Chairman Charles Goodell publicly stated that he would not work two years to trade an undesirable discharge for a clemency discharge, and thousands of applicants agreed with him. Nor were many who applied to the Clemency Board eager to do an apparently nominal period of work to earn clemency. Some had originally applied with the hope that they would be among those granted immediate, unconditional relief; when they were not, they dropped out of the program.

(2) The Defense Department's "loophole" and the Justice Department's continuing dismissals of cases produced thousands of alternative service dropouts. Many military fugitives signed up for clemency only as a way to end their fugitive status, and they never intended to follow through with alternative service. A smaller number of draft fugitives dropped out of the program when their attorneys were able to convince federal prosecutors to drop all charges against them.

(3) The lack of follow-through in the program's administration reinforced many applicants' disinterest in the program. The Clemency Board had personal contact with only a handful of its 15,500 cases, so its applicants were given little stimulus to contact Selective Service and look for an acceptable job.* Similarly, the De-

---

*The impact of the Clemency Board's lack of personal contact can be demonstrated by its applicants' failure to make any contact with Selective Service. Only 45 percent of the Board's applicants did so, versus 82 percent of the Defense Department applicants who had been given much

fense Department maintained no contact of any kind with applicants after they left the Joint Clemency Processing Center
in Indiana. With each Selective Service state headquarters
trimmed back to just the state director, the late stages of the
president's program were administered almost entirely by cor-
respondence.

Even if President Ford's program had been more generous
and better administered, alternative service would still have
been a disappointment. It was just not a realistic condition.
Public service had been a reasonable requirement for conscientious objectors during the Vietnam War, but they were well-
motivated people who were working at their jobs at the same
time their peers were fighting in Vietnam. After the war ended,
their interest in staying with alternative service began to erode.
Many might have been prosecuted for quitting their jobs, had
Selective Service not summarily terminated alternative service
in November 1974.

Clemency applicants were much less likely than Vietnam-era
conscientious objectors to find and hold a job. Most military offenders had, in effect, quit their jobs in the service when they
committed their original violations. Many were disadvantaged,
with no skills and poor work habits. Even those who were cap-
able of finding and keeping a job sometimes found alternative
service incompatible with their present circumstances. They
were approaching thirty and had steady jobs and growing families to support. When they were unable to find economically
supporting alternative service work they gave up and dropped
out of the program.

Of the 13,300 people assigned to alternative service, 8,400
people (63 percent) signed up with Selective Service, 4,500
(34 percent) began acceptable jobs, and 2,500 (19 percent)
appear likely to complete the program. The Justice Department
phase will have the highest percentage of completions (about
70 percent) because of the likelihood that dropouts will be
prosecuted. The Clemency Board phase will have only 25 percent complete the program, a disappointing figure in light of
the very short assignments given most of its applicants. The
Defense Department phase will have the lowest percentage (10
percent), probably because of the "loophole."

---

longer alternative service assignments. Apparently, the in-person counseling given Defense Department applicants convinced them to make personal
contact with Selective Service.

Those who stayed with the program did so for a variety of reasons. People who were originally unemployed saw alternative service as a way of finding a job. Others were able to get credit for staying on jobs they already held. Those who were fugitive draft offenders were eager to escape prosecution for their original offenses. Finally, some have been working under the false impression that the benefits will be greater than they really are or that they face legal punishment if they quit. Occasionally, these misimpressions resulted from conversations with Selective Service officials, many of whom were very ill-informed about the clemency program.

Local Selective Service officials acknowledge that the main benefit of alternative service has been to find jobs for a handful of unemployed people. Beyond that, its greatest impact has been to cut by almost 11,000 the number of individuals who received clemency under the Ford plan.

Overall Assessment

The results of the Ford program have come as a disappointment to those who had hoped that a conditional plan patterned after the original Taft-Koch proposals would solve the amnesty problem.

Critics of the Ford program usually point to the low participation as proof of the program's failure. The numbers are striking, but standing alone they do not necessarily indicate that the program was faulty. If the president's offer had been realistic, if it had been administered evenhandedly, and if everyone had a fair chance to take advantage of it, the rate might indicate nothing more than the unwillingness of Vietnam-era offenders to participate in a national reconciliation. But the clemency program had such major defects in design and administration that the low numbers reflect more on it than on the people it purported to help.

There are many reasons why the Ford program never lived up to expectations. Its tone was too punitive, its conditions too unrealistic, and its benefits too meager. Its case-by-case procedures were complex and expensive. Its public information campaign was inadequate to overcome the general confusion about who was eligible to apply. Above all, the clemency it offered was no better, and in some ways worse, than relief that was available through normal government channels.

But these were not the root problems. They were just sympto-
matic of the more fundamental weaknesses of the Ford program:
it was (1) an awkward compromise, (2) based on serious misconceptions about Vietnam-era offenders, (3) suffering from a near-
total lack of planning, (4) unsupervised authority given to the
wrong federal agencies, and (5) insufficient presidential involvement.

(1) The "clemency" concept was an awkward compromise
heavily influenced by the political environment of the early
1970s. President Ford offered limited, conditional, case-by-case
clemency as a middle ground between unlimited, unconditional,
blanket amnesty and nothing at all. The concept gave many
Americans the mistaken impression that a solution had been
found, temporarily putting the emotional amnesty issue to rest.
In practice, though, the compromise bore little relationship to
the real policy problems of the amnesty issue.

(2) The President's initial speech about clemency before the
VFW convention in August 1974 focused attention on the clasic
images of "draft evader" and "deserter." Thereafter, his program
was designed around the misconception that draft and military
offenders were like the conscientious objectors of the late
sixties: well-educated, middle-calss war resisters. They were
thought to be part of an antiwar, amnesty network, and flexible
enough in their future plans to be able to do alternative service
without inordinate sacrifice. In fact, this image applied to very
few.

(3) The program suffered from inadequate planning. When
Mr. Ford assumed the Presidency, his staff immediately looked
for policy papers on the subject prepared by the Nixon administration. All they found was a Defense Department study of
AWOL and desertion which had never been intended to help a
president make decisions about amnesty. Despite this lack of
staffwork, President Ford committed himself to the concept of
"earned reentry" in his speech at the VFW convention. After
the speech, and especially after the Nixon pardon, the president
was under considerable public pressure to announce the specifics
of his program quickly. There was no time to conduct an inquiry into the background and status of Vietnam-era offenders.
Instead, the White House staff had to work out the details of
the program with officials from Justice, Defense, and Selective
Service based on *ad hoc* impressions about what the policy

problems really were. No plans were made to account for foreseeable difficulties.

(4) Because of the absence of planning, the White House staff had to rely heavily on the advice of the Justice Department, Defense Department, and Selective Service. At the urging of these agencies, the White House rejected the idea of having a specially established Clemency Board administer the entire program. Instead, the program was decentralized, with the Clemency Board having jurisdiction over aspects of the program in which other agencies had no interest. As a result, the program was run largely by the same federal agencies against whom draft and military offenders had already rebelled. These young men were expected to overcome their deep-seated antagonisms toward the military, federal prosecutors, and draft boards and to assume that they would be treated compassionately under the clemency program. At the same time, officials in those agencies were expected to overcome what were often intensely hostile attitudes toward the offenders. But the deeper problem was the tendency of the Justice Department and Defense Department to tailor the program to their own institutional needs, principally their desire to trim backlogs of fugitive cases while maintaining the appearance of stern enforcement of the law.

(5) The clemency program was the result of President Ford's personal convictions. These were convictions not shared by members of his staff or the rest of his administration. They believed that the president's decision had been a mistake, so they tried to minimize its political consequences. Upon their urging, President Ford rarely associated himself in any public way with his clemency initiative. His program could have been more popular, better understood, and more effectively administered if the president had assumed a more visible role. Unfortunately, this vacuum could not be filled by any other Ford administration spokesman, since no one was publicly responsible for the entire clemency program. The most visible spokesman was Clemency Board Chairman Charles Goodell, but he had authority only for the board itself and could not speak for the overall program.

For all its defects, the Ford program was an important step toward the resolution of the amnesty issue. Before it was implemented, amnesty had been addressed only in political and hypothetical terms. Very little was then known about the real

problems of draft and military offenders. One can easily criti-
cize the Ford program for its flaws in emphasis, design, and administration—but many of those mistakes resulted from the
limited information and the political environment which existed
at the time. Through the Ford program, considerable data was
generated about Vietnam-era draft and military offenders, and
the Defense Department and Clemency Board issued comprehensive public reports. A new program can profit from the mistakes
of the Ford clemency program, while taking advantage of the
greater understanding of the issue which it produced.

4. A Program of Relief for Vietnam-Era Draft and Military Offenders

Despite the good intentions and original high hopes of the Ford clemency program, it was not a sufficient response to the needs of draft and military offenders. Something more must be done.

Four fundamental characteristics are essential for any program to be a success:

It should be realistic in its assessment of offenders' current status and probable future plans.

It should offer substantial practical relief fashioned to meet the legal and personal needs of individuals in differing circumstances.

It should be nonvindictive and nonpunitive, making no judgment about the rightness or wrongness of anyone's actions.

It should be fair to all individuals in light of their personal circumstances, their offenses, their prior service, and their punishments.

Presented below are recommendations for a comprehensive program of relief for Vietnam-era offenders, along with a discussion of the issues which underlie these recommendations.

Policy decisions have to be made in a number of separate areas: eligibility, nature of relief, conditions, method of case review, categories of individuals, and implementation.

Eligibility

Period of Coverage

Setting any limitation on the period of coverage involves a measure of inequity. Many draft and military violations during the Vietnam era were no different from those committed in earlier years nor from those which are still being committed today. Thousands of Americans have tarnished reputations arising out of World War I, World War II, the Korean War, and the pre-Vietnam cold war. Their lives have been irreparably affected by their felony records and bad discharges. Excluding them from a post-Vietnam program raises difficult questions of equity. However, the justification for having any program has always been the Vietnam War and its damaging side effects. Relief for offenders of other eras should not be included in a post-Vietnam program. It should be part of more comprehensive reforms in draft and military discharge policies, instead.

The time jurisdiction of President Ford's clemency program was defined by the passage of the Gulf of Tonkin Resolution (August 4, 1964), marking the formal beginning of American involvement in Vietnam, and the date of withdrawal of American combat troops (March 28, 1973), marking the end of American combat responsibilities. This is a logical definition of the Vietnam era, yet it excludes many individuals who were Vietnam-era draftees or draft-induced enlistees. It also excludes a few draft and military offenders whose conduct was directly affected by a war which actually lasted from 1961 to 1975. These individuals should be included in the program.

> *Recommendation 1:*
> The program should encompass all qualifying civilian military offenses occurring between August 4, 1964, and March 28, 1973. Offenses occurring outside this designated period should be included if (1) they were committed by draftees or draft-induced enlistees subsequent to March 28, 1973; (2) they occurred in Southeast Asia; or (3) they were motivated by opposition to American policies in Southeast Asia.

Qualifying Offenses

A program for Vietnam-era offenders should encompass all non-violent offenses which were reasonably related to the Vietnam War. Vietnam-related offenses such as bombings, burglaries, assaults, fraggings, and vandalism should not be covered. Official forgiveness should not be extended to individuals who demonstrated this kind of disregard for the safety and property of others. The line between violent and nonviolent offenses can easily be determined, but defining which actions were Vietnam-related is much more difficult. The impact of the war was far-reaching. It extended far beyond those who refused induction or refused to report for Vietnam and influenced the behavior of many more than those who explicitly attributed their offenses to the war. Even an individual review of every case would not identify those offenses which were precisely associated with Vietnam. However, broad categories of war-related offenses can be designated. Case-by-case determinations should be employed only where necessary to prevent a gross overinclusion of offenses which obviously had nothing to do with the war.

For civilians, the program should encompass all violations of the Selective Service Act which involve an individual's failure to cooperate with the draft—such as nonregistration, failure to report for induction, or destroying one's own draft card. It also should include offenses which had no relationship to an individual's own draft status, such as nonviolent acts of civil disobedience and refusal to pay taxes, but only after case-by-case determinations that each individual had been motivated by opposition to the war.

For military offenders, it should cover absence offenses and other violations of military discipline which would not be crimes in the civilian community. These include such nonviolent misconduct as disrespect to an officer, disobedience to orders, mutiny, sedition, and uttering disloyal statements. Conduct which would be criminal in a civilian context, such as fraud, sale of dangerous drugs, and violence to persons or property should not be covered by the program. However, the use and possession of drugs should be a qualifying offense, even though it is also a crime in civilian society. The widespread drug-abuse problem in the services was originally regarded as a purely criminal matter. The military came to recognize drug use as a medical problem, qualifying soldiers for general discharges. Later, the Defense Department instituted a discharge revision program to upgrade the bad discharges of persons separated for drug abuse before this change in policy. This policy should be incorporated in this new program.

An important distinction should be made between persons discharged for alleged criminal conduct and those actually convicted of criminal acts. Individuals who were offered and who accepted administrative undesirable discharges were never convicted of any offense. They cannot properly be assumed to have been guilty of the charges, and their military files are often so incomplete that a fair conclusion cannot always be drawn about the strength of the evidence against them. Regardless of the charges which prompted their separations, all persons with undesirable discharges must be included in the program.

The fact that an individual may have committed a qualifying offense should not automatically guarantee him any relief. Certain offenses may have occurred under particularly serious circumstances, requiring a careful review of the individual's case.* A case-by-case review would also be necessary to distinguish war-related civil disobedience or tax offenses from offenses of the same type which were motivated by other causes.

Even if an individual qualifies for the program in all other respects, a question arises whether he should be disqualified if his record discloses any military, federal, or state conviction for a serious felony crime unrelated to his draft or military offenses. Relief under the program would be extended only for qualifying draft and military offenses, and its denial might be considered a form of double jeopardy. However, granting relief to persons convicted of such serious crimes as murder or rape might jeopardize the program's goal of reconciliation. A thorough check into criminal justice records would be necessary to idenitfy these individuals.**

> *Recommendation 2:*
> The program should encompass all civilian and military offenses which were nonviolent and reasonably related to the Vietnam War. For civilians, this includes such

---

*See pages 69–72 for a discussion of which case would be given case-by-case review.

**Without conducting a records check, the Clemency Board discovered that about 12 percent of its military applicants and 4 percent of its civilian applicants had felony conviction records.

offenses as (1) failure to cooperate with the draft; (2) destruction of one's own draft card; (3) nonviolent civil disobedience; and (4) failure to pay taxes. For servicemen, this includes (1) absence offenses; (2) other offenses against military discipline; and (3) any offenses which resulted in administrative undesirable discharges.

Recommendation 3:
No serviceman discharged by court-martial for a civilian-type crime or still facing general court-martial charges for a civilian-type crime should be eligible for relief.

Recommendation 4:
No person convicted in any state, federal, or military court of a serious felony crime should be eligible for relief.

Nature of Relief

Perhaps the major issue to be determined in any amnesty program is the nature of the relief that would be offered. There are four major types of relief which should be part of any comprehensive program—pardons, military discharges, veterans' benefits, and changes in official records.

Pardons

Throughout the public debate over amnesty for Vietnam-era offenders, there has been much dispute over the distinction between "amnesty" and "pardon." Some suggest that an amnesty forgets, while a pardon forgives; others say that an amnesty is directed is directed to classes of individuals, whereas pardons are directed to the individuals themselves. Most of these disagreements have been more political than legal in nature. Either term may be used to characterize a program of relief.

Regardless of how a program is characterized, a pardon is a necessary legal remedy for individuals with federal convictions. A pardon is the highest expression of executive clemency authorized by the Constitution, yet it is a flexible remedy which can be tailored to the objectives of any program. A pardon may be granted as an act of compassion, as a recognition of rehabilitation, as an acknowledgment of a miscarriage of justice, or as any other expression of forgiveness.

However, a pardon standing alone is not a sufficient form of relief. It has two serious weaknesses: Its legal and practical effects are limited, and it is widely considered to reflect an admission of guilt.

The legal impact of a pardon is not as great as commonly thought. A pardon restores most federal civil rights lost by reason of a conviction—voting rights, eligibility for elective office or jury service, and a few other matters. However, an offense, although pardoned, can still bar an alien from American citizenship or deny a former serviceman an upgrade of his military discharge. The most important impact of a pardon is the removal of civil disabilities imposed by state law. A person with a federal conviction often loses state civil rights, restricting his eligibility for state employment, state assistance programs, and occupational licenses. Ordinarily, a presidential pardon removes these state-imposed disabilities.

Regardless of the restoration of these civil rights, the recipient of a pardon is still subject to the social and economic hardships which accompany a felony conviction. The fact of conviction must often be acknowledged. For this reason a pardon should be accompanied by supplemental relief to help individuals overcome the adverse effects of their convictions.*

To give pardons greater effect, the president should specify what he has in mind by granting them. President Ford did not do this. Instead, he issued undefined "full and unconditional" pardons, enabling the recipients, courts, government agencies, and the public to interpret them in different ways. The Veterans Administration and military discharge review boards have given Ford's pardons very little effect, and it remains unclear whether pardon recipients must acknowledge their conviction records on federal employment applications. Pardons issued under a new program should be accompanied by a presidential statement informing recipients of the rights and benefits that the pardons convey, prescribing how government agencies must interpret them, and advising the public about what the pardons mean.

The pardon's connotation of guilt is a more difficult problem to overcome. Like a deed or gift, a pardon must be accepted by the recipient to be effective. Traditionally, pardons have been

*See pages 61–63 for a discussion of the need to change and seal official records.

issued to those who have already been convicted, and the acceptance of a pardon has come to signify a personal acknowledgment
of guilt. This principle has support in case law and is the official position of the U.S. pardon attorney. It is also a view widely
accepted by many proponents of amnesty, who interpret pardons as reflecting the official judgment that morally culpable
acts have been committed.

There is no reason why a pardon must be viewed as an acknowledgment of wrongdoing or a reflection of the motivations
which may have prompted the recipient's conduct. However, a
pardon is an acknowledgment of the fact that the law was broken,
and it does not affect the legal validity of the original conviction. Otherwise, a pardon might support a legal claim for remedial
relief for the disabilities suffered as a result of that conviction.

Any pardon given an unconvicted person operates as a complete grant of immunity from future prosecution. However, because a pardon is an admission of legal guilt, it is not a suitable
form of relief for persons who have only been accused but not
convicted of draft charges. Under American law, no individual
is considered guilty until convicted according to due process of
law. Given the great difficulties which federal prosecutors have
had in obtaining draft convictions recently, every draft fugitive
has an excellent chance to have his case dismissed or acquitted
if he stands trial. Although there are many practical considera-
tions which would lead an individual to avoid a trial, acceptance
of the pardon reflects his acknowledgment that he would be
convicted.

Since the pardon inescapably suggests that the government
considers the charge legally well founded, its offer to persons
whose guilt has not been established would create confusion
about the motives of the government. This could detract from
the broader, nonvindictive goals of a new program. Considering
the widespread view in the pro-amnesty community that a pardon implies moral guilt, offering pardons to unconvicted persons might provoke a boycott, with many people choosing to
remain liable to prosecution rather than make such an admission.

All of these problems can be avoided by rejecting the use of
the pardon in favor of the equally effective and less controversial
act of simply dismissing outstanding charges. The government
can decline to prosecute unindicted cases at its discretion, seek

dismissal of indictments by the court, or refuse to oppose motions for acquittal by the defendants. None of these alternatives could be interpreted as inferring either legal or moral culpability.

A new program should avoid the issuance of pardons in military cases except for servicemen convicted by special or general courts-martial, who suffer the same disabilities as civilians convicted of federal offenses. The Clemency Board offered pardons to all its military applicants, including those who had not been convicted by court-martial, because of its conclusion that the clemency discharge had no practical and little, if any, symbolic value. The board concluded that the presidential pardon had a greater symbolic value and could be understood as forgiving the underlying conduct which had led to the administrative separation. In a more comprehensive program of relief, there would be no reason to issue pardons to servicemen who were discharged administratively.

> *Recommendation 5:*
> Pardons should be the form of relief issued to convicted civilian offenders and servicemen who were convicted by general or special courts-martial. The issuance of pardons should be accompanied by a clear presidential explanation of their intended legal and social effects.

> *Recommendation 6:*
> Pardons are not the appropriate form of relief for those charged with, but not convicted of, a draft offense. Pending draft charges should simply be dismissed.

Military Discharges

Traditionally, the armed forces have issued discharges which characterize the quality of service of individuals released from the military. There are now five different kinds of discharges. In recent years, over nine-tenths of all discharges have been honorable discharges. The general discharge is also given "under honorable conditions," but reflects a judgment that the soldier's performance did not warrant a fully honorable certificate. Both honorable and general discharges convey entitlement to veterans' benefits under present law.

Undesirable and bad-conduct discharges are given "under other-than-honorable conditions," reflecting unsatisfactory ser-

vice. The undesirable discharge is issued by administrative procedures not involving court-martial. A bad-conduct discharge is a
more severe sanction, which is only issued following conviction
by court-martial.* It is often adjudged by special courts-martial
which have jurisdiction over minor offenses carrying a maximum
penalty of no more than six months confinement. The dishonorable discharge, issued "under dishonorable conditions," may
only be imposed upon conviction by a general court-martial for
a very serious offense. It is an automatic disqualification for
veterans' benefits. As a general matter, bad-conduct and undesirable discharges disqualify recipients from veterans' benefits.**

The armed forces place great value on their ability to characterize military service. They consider the honorable discharge to
be an important incentive to good performance, and the risk of
receiving a lesser discharge to be a deterrent to misconduct. The
most obvious reward is eligibility for veterans' benefits, but much
of a discharge's value also stems from the weight it carries in society. Servicemen are counseled that the type of discharge they
receive will have lasting impact on their lives. It is questionable,
however, whether this impact is appreciated by the average soldier
Those who are unwilling or unable to perform satisfactorily are
often just interested in being discharged as quickly as possible.
They experience the consequences of their discharge type only
after they return to civilian life, when they must contend with
the social and economic disabilities entailed by all but the fully
honorable discharge. This stigma is complicated by public confusion about what each discharge means. The common tendency
is to view all discharges other than honorable as a reflection of
poor service and bad character.

The Ford clemency program fashioned relief outside the existing discharge structure, but its "clemency discharge" was unsatisfactory for three reasons. First, it was a newly created discharge
having no established meaning; it was designed solely to indicate
that an individual had received clemency under the president's
program. Second, it was officially considered be "under-other-

---

*Curiously, the bad-conduct discharge is sometimes considered better
than the undesirable discharge by people who do not understand the military discharge structure. "Bad conduct" suggests minor misconduct, while
"undesirable" implies permanent character defects.

**Holders of undesirable and bad-conduct discharges are eligible to
apply to the Veterans Administration for veterans' benefits. Almost always,
they are turned down.

than-honorable conditions," thereby effecting no change in the character of discharge originally issued to most people covered by the program. Finally, it singled out its recipients as "deserters," since they were the only ones who hold this type of discharge. The experience with clemency discharges demonstrates that any meaningful relief must involve working within the existing discharge structure by granting honorable or general discharges.

Such relief would be consistent with the post-Vietnam liberalization of discharge policies by the armed forces. Through their expeditious and trainee discharge programs, they now offer honorable or general discharges to individuals who are not performing satisfactorily—the same people who previously would have received bad discharges. They automatically upgrade discharges for Vietnam-era servicemen who had been punished for drug use. Their discharge review boards now grant about one-third of all applications for upgrades. In the army, half of those who appear in person are successful.

Granting Vietnam-era offenders honorable discharges would eliminate all distinctions between them and soldiers who performed well under conditions which were difficult for everyone. In effect, this would involve a fundamental rejection of the military discharge structure. It would impair the value of an honorable discharge, which the armed forces and many Americans believe to be an important symbol of meritorious service to the country.

The general discharge is a preferable, if not totally satisfactory alternative. Granting general discharges to Vietnam-era offenders might impair the social status of the 300,000 veterans who already hold general discharges. Also, the general discharge carries a definite stigma, since it is not fully honorable. But "general discharge" does not have the negative connotations of the words "undesirable," "bad conduct," or "dishonorable," and several studies have shown that it is a less severe handicap in the job market. Through public statements, the appropriate federal authorities should request all Americans, and especially employers, not to discriminate against veterans with general discharges.

Some cases may warrant honorable discharges. For example, individuals were sometimes sent home to await further orders only to be charged with AWOL and given a bad discharge. Others were denied hardship leave despite extraordinary family problems and then were punished for unauthorized absences.* Former

---

*The Clemency Board found that 14 percent of its military cases involved some procedural unfairness.

servicemen covered by this program should retain the right to seek further relief through existing military discharge review boards.

> *Recommendation 7:*
> General discharges should be the form of relief issued to military offenders.

> *Recommendation 8:*
> All former servicemen should retain the opportunity to apply for an honorable discharge through military discharge review boards.

Veterans' Benefits

Granting general discharges would ordinarily confer automatic eligibility for veterans' benefits to all recipients who served six months or more on active duty. This would provide opportunities for job training and employment services, helping to overcome the economic disabilities former servicemen have suffered in the years since they received their original discharges. A uniform policy of this type would treat veterans' benefits as a social-welfare program, not a form of compensation for service to the country. However, this would be contrary to the traditional justification for veterans' benefits. Vietnam-era military offenders should be relieved of enduring stigmas, but that does not mean that they should be rewarded with full veterans' benefits for service they did not in fact perform.

The Ford clemency program explicitly directed that no recipient of clemency would thereby become entitled to veterans' benefits. By doing so, it excluded an important form of relief for thousands of former servicemen who had clearly earned these benefits. Over 25 percent of the Clemency Board's applicants had served in Vietnam, and many others had long periods of good military service. The Defense Department clemency program found that 18 percent of its applicants were Vietnam veterans, many of whom had fought with distinction.

The question of discharge type should be separated from the question of benefits. General discharges should be granted widely, but veterans' benefits should be restricted to former servicemen who clearly earned them. Individuals who served full Vietnam tours, or partial tours which ended in injury, did what was expected of them and should receive full benefits. Individuals who suffered service-incurred injuries deserve medical care for the treatment of those injuries even if they do no necessarily deserve full veterans' benefits. If these standards were applied, approximately 25 percent of the 250,000 Vietnam-era military offenders would qualify for benefits. Distinctions of this kind could be established through a clerical file review, and no case-by-case discretionary decision-making would be needed.

However, the cases of servicemen with extended periods of military service should not be overlooked. Some had already established their entitlement for veterans' benefits in earlier enlistments, only to lose those benefits through subsequent offenses. Some had served for so long and committed such minor offenses that they clearly warrant veterans' benefits. Other cases are much less sympathetic. Since no blanket rule is possible, a case-by-case review should be extended to each individual who served two years or more in the armed forces, the same length of time draftees had to serve. This review should take place through normal Veterans Administration channels upon individual application, but according to special standards set by the presidential task force implementing this program. Approximately 25 percent of all military offenders would be eligible to apply for this review.

The limited and categorical approach of this program should not preclude the granting of individually tailored relief through normal channels. Anyone who did not satisfy the special conditions for veterans' benefits should still be able to apply to the Veterans Administration for review under existing standards.

A general discharge with these distinctions regarding veterans' benefits can be created by the president under the authority of Article II, Section 2 of the Constitution or under existing authority.* If these distinctions are not made, then either of the following unpleasant choices would have to be adopted: veterans' benefits would have to be given to individuals who never earned them or servicemen would have to be left with their original bad discharges.

*The Ford Clemency Program's creation of a new type of discharge and the scope of the President's pardon power interpreted by *Schick* v. *Reed,* 419 U.S. 256 (1974), and *Hoffa* v. *Saxbe,* 378 F. Supp. 1221 (D.C.D.C. 1974), provides support for the president's constitutional authority.

Statutes governing the issuance of discharges and entitlement to veterans' benefits give the president authority to determine the form and legal effect of the discharge. The same result could also be achieved by legislation.

Recommendation 9:
Entitlement to full veterans' benefits should be extended only to former servicemen who served a Vietnam tour which did not end because of misconduct. Former servicemen not otherwise entitled to benefits who have service-connected injuries should be granted medical benefits only. (This requires new legislation.)

Recommendation 10:
The Veterans Administration should review applications for veterans' benefits from individuals with two years or more of military service under standards especially established for this program.

Recommendation 11:
All former servicemen should retain the opportunity to apply for veterans' benefits through the Veterans Administration.

Changes in Official Records

Relief must be accompanied by conforming changes in official records. This involves a major administrative task but one which is necessary for the program to have a significant effect on people's lives.

New discharges forms should be issued to former servicemen to replace the bad discharges they now hold. General-discharge certificates should include no explicit information that they were granted as part of this program. However, the provisions of this program would subject the specially issued general discharges to stricter veterans' benefits entitlement standards than is true for all other general discharges. The Veterans Administration must therefore have some means for looking behind the discharge in order to determine entitlement for benefits.

Arrest records of unconvicted draft offenders should be destroyed. Steps must be taken to remove all records of pardoned offenses from public scrutiny. Records of federal convictions are kept on file in local courts and in several federal criminal information systems. They are available on request to federal and state law-enforcement agencies and sometimes to other government agencies. The widespread accessibility of these records to government sources sometimes results in their dissemination to nongovernmental employers and other private institutions. Because federal court records are open to the general public, many credit information agencies take note of indictment and conviction records.

The most complete and permanent approach to the problem of indictment and conviction records lies in the purging or erasure of evidence of the criminal record. A number of convicted draft offenders have had relief of this nature under the Federal Youth Corrections Act. The complete purging of conviction records seems to be an extreme remedy which precludes access to this information even for national security and other important government purposes. While a pardoned draft or military offense should not act as a general bar to government employment, it may be a valid basis for disqualifying someone from exercising responsibilities of a very sensitive nature. For this reason, sealing is a more desirable means of restricting access to conviction records. The sealing policy should permit the conviction record to be obtained only for such matters as security checks or appointments to sensitive government positions. Apart from these exceptions, individuals should never be required to reveal their sealed records when seeking employment, credit, or other social privileges.

Records maintained by the executive branch remain in the control of the Justice Department and the armed forces. For this reason, a decision to seal federal conviction information may be done by executive direction, with the president setting whatever terms he thinks necessary. Still, the powers of the president and the attorney general do not extend to records maintained by the courts or the private sector. In order to seal these other records, legislative action would be necessary.

All relief granted by the program should be accompanied by action to conform official records to the new status of program beneficiaries. Records should be changed and sealed at the government's own initiative. However, the government should notify all individuals about the relief granted them, the changes in their official records, and the new rights and benefits available. About half of all beneficiaries can be reached through direct mailings to last known addresses. In addition, there should be a major public-information campaign through the media and regional offices of designated federal agencies to advise people who cannot be reached by mail.

Recommendation 12:

General discharges should be issued to replace existing discharges and must include no indication that they were issued pursuant to this program. The Veterans Administration must have an independent means of determining whether a general discharge was issued pursuant to this program in order to establish entitlement to veterans' benefits.

Recommendation 13:

Arrest records of unconvicted civilians should be destroyed. Records of civilian indictments and convictions and military court-martial convictions should be sealed, with use carefully restricted to designated purposes. Individuals should not be required to reveal the existence of these records. (This requires new legislation.)

Recommendation 14:

Changes in official records should be made at the government's own initiative. Individuals should be personally notified about the changes in their status. These efforts should be supplemented by public information campaigns.

Conditions of Relief

In the Ford program, individuals had to satisfy certain conditions before they were granted relief. They had to apply before a fixed deadline, sign an oath of allegiance (except at the Clemency Board), and perform a period of alternative service. Other amnesty proposals have suggested that an individual seeking relief must assert or prove that his conduct was motivated by conscientious opposition to the Vietnam War.

None of these four conditions is realistic or advisable in the overwhelming majority of cases. Individuals who are unworthy of relief should simply be excluded, not subjected to conditions which undermine the effectiveness of the entire program. Except for a few special circumstances, there should be no conditions in the new program.

Applications

Government programs of all kinds have difficulty in informing people about their eligibility for benefits. Usually, it takes

years for news about a federal program to seep down to people
who are affected by it. At the start, people do not know that a
new program exists, they do not know it includes them, they
do not know how to apply or are never motivated to apply.
These circumstances are especially important when the people
to be reached are socially or economically disadvantaged. The
motivational problem is particularly severe among groups whose
prior experience with the government resulted in punishment
or the serious risk of punishment. For all of these reasons, the
main effect of requiring applications from draft and military
offenders is to exclude those who are too uninformed, confused,
or afraid to apply.

If applications were required, the eligibility period would have
to last for years, buttressed by extensive information programs
designed to contact eligible people. The experience of the Ford
program suggests that widespread advertising could have a substantial impact on the level of applications. But despite the program's six and one-half month application period and three-
month public information campaign, about 500 individuals applied late because they did not learn of their eligibility in time.
Today, veterans counselors still encounter people who never
knew that they could apply. A year after the start of the Ford
program, a Gallup poll found that only 15 percent of the American public knew that the program included "deserters" with bad
discharges, by far the largest group of eligible persons. It is reasonable to assume that a significant number of potential applicants would not have been reached no matter how long the
program had been open.

There are advantages in requiring applications when the
program deals with individuals on a case-by-case basis and
involves a significant amount of discretion in affording relief. People can then be more easily located, informed of their
rights, and invited to participate in the review of their cases.
But these advantages do not outweigh the culling-out effect of
requiring applications when individuals can be identified as members of eligible categories through review of existing government
records, and when there would be very little variation in the relief offered. They need only be given an opportunity to submit
information on their own behalf and informed of the action the
government has taken in their cases.

However, three categories of persons should be required to

apply, either because of the impossibility of identifying their cases from among all government records or because their cases require individual review which would be impossible without their participation: (1) those whose offenses occurred outside the designated 1964–73 period, (2) those who were convicted for tax offenses motivated by their opposition to the war, and (3) those with substantial military service who seek veterans' benefits.

> *Recommendation 15:*
> Participation in the program should not require individual application except for (1) persons whose offenses occurred outside the designated 1964–73 period; (2) persons who were convicted of tax offenses motivated by opposition to the war; and (3) persons with extended periods of military service who seek veterans' benefits. All other eligible individuals would be identified through a search of appropriate records.

Alternative Service

A key feature of the Ford program was its requirement that individuals perform a period of alternative service as a condition of obtaining relief. The premise behind this condition was that these individuals had unfulfilled obligations of service which had to be satisfied. However, the experience of the Ford program proved that it is unrealistic to impose requirements of service on individuals who earlier demonstrated an inability or unwillingness to fulfill comparable obligations.

The original idea of alternative service arose in the 1971 Taft bill, which envisioned amnesty as a second chance for would-be conscientious objectors to do civilian service instead of going to war. The proposal was made at a time when thousands of COs were doing service of one kind or another, and offenders were pictured as being little different from ordinary COs. By the time the Ford program was announced, the people asked to do service were in their late twenties, ill-inclined to interrupt their lives to fulfill any lingering obligation from the Vietnam era. Some were reluctant to give up steady jobs. Others regarded alternative service as punishment, tantamount to an admission that they had wrongfully avoided service. Above all, two years

was generally considered to be more of a *quid pro quo* than
was warranted by the clemency offered in return. This resistance contributed to the Ford program's low application rate
and to its dropout rate among those who were assigned alternative service.

Even if a new program offered more benefits than the Ford
program, imposing a condition of alternative service would dis-
courage most people from participating. Today, prospective participants are older and even less likely to be willing to interrupt their lives than when President Ford created his program.
The war is now two more years behind us. Furthermore, imposing such a condition would perpetuate much of the bitter-
ness of the Vietnam era. Not only would many Vietnam-era
offenders resent the condition, but some critics would probably
resist any effort to find employment for this group of individuals while the unemployment rate for honorably discharged
Vietnam veterans is so high. Many members of the public
might wrongly interpret failure to complete assigned service
as further proof of unworthiness. Finally, alternative service
would either have to be imposed uniformly or a vast bureau-
cracy akin to the Clemency Board would have to be established
to make assignments through expensive and time-consuming
case-by-case review. The administration of an alternative service requirement would be expensive and fraught with bureau-
cratic difficulties.

> *Recommendation 16:*
> No form of alternative service should be required.

Oath of Allegiance

The Ford clemency program required returning fugitives to
sign a reaffirmation of allegiance when they applied for clemency. This oath was described by Attorney General Saxbe as
an "act of contrition" and was based on the idea that Vietnam-
era draft or military offenses were acts of questionable patrio-
tism, casting doubt on an individual's loyalty and allegiance.

Any special oath would be offensive to many participants,
and it would subject others to some legal risks, Many Vietnam-
era offenders have permanent homes in Canada, Sweden, or
elsewhere. While they would like to settle their legal status

with the United States, signing an oath of allegiance might jeopardize their rights in their adopted countries. By affirming their allegiance to the United States, they would raise questions about their allegiance to the countries whose citizenship they already hold or may someday seek.

Special oaths have no place in a program which is designed to be neutral on the moral issues of the war or the conduct of the offenders. For this reason, the only circumstance in which an oath should be required is for an individual who accepted foreign citizenship and wishes to reestablish his American citizenship. This oath should be no different from that required by law of every other new citizen.*

> *Recommendation 17:*
> No oath or acknowledgment of allegiance should be imposed except for those seeking to restore American citizenship.

Test of Conscience

Many proposals for amnesty have limited relief to those who assert or prove that their offenses were motivated by antiwar sentiments. The Ford program, however, imposed no test of conscience as a condition of eligibility. Such proposals reflect a fundamental misunderstanding of the diverse nature of Vietnam-era offenders. They tend to exclude individuals with poor educational or social backgrounds, reinforcing the patterns of class discrimination that existed during the draft. Establishing such a motivation would raise many of the difficulties encountered by local draft boards in determining the sincerity of conscientious objectors during the Vietnam War. It would give an enormous advantage to articulate, well-counseled people. Most case records are so skimpy that it would be impossible for an individual to prove or for the government to disprove that an offense had been related to an individual's antiwar feelings. Yet if all that is required is a perfunctory declaration of prior antiwar beliefs, no real purpose would be

*Under present law, one may, for conscientious reasons, refuse to take that part of the oath which promises to bear arms in defense of the country.

served. People would simply be tempted to make false declarations, turning the requirement into a charade.

Aside from its impracticality, a test of conscience is undesirable because it would preserve the myth that individuals who avoided the draft or performed unsatisfactory military service did so just for one reason—opposition to the war. Above all, it would reflect an implicit judgment about the morality of the war by construing all offenders as conscientious objectors. For these reasons, test of conscience or motivation should ordinarily not be a condition of eligibility for the program.

However, a test of conscience would serve a useful purpose if it were employed to determine the basic eligibility of the following three special categories of offenders: (1) individuals whose offense occurred outside the designated 1964–73 period, (2) those convicted of nonviolent war-related acts of civil disobedience, and (3) those convicted of war-related tax offenses. Absent some means to establish motivation, these individuals could not be encompassed in the program without also including common tax offenders and persons who committed civil disobedience for every imaginable cause.

The difficulties of implementing such a test remain, and these cases would have to be reviewed with particular care. Something more than a mere assertion of antiwar motivation should be required. Either the antiwar character of the offense must be plain from official records, or else the individual must submit corroborative statements or other evidence to support his assertions.

Finally, motivation is relevant in making case-by-case determinations as to whether military offenses were so serious that relief should be denied. Conscientious reasons for an offense should be weighed in an individual's favor.

Recommendation 18:
No test of conscience should be employed except to establish the eligibility of (1) persons whose offenses occurred outside the designated 1964–73 period; (2) persons convicted of nonviolent acts of civil disobedience motivated by opposition to the war; and (3) persons convicted of tax offenses motivated by opposition to the war.

Method of Case Review

Merits of the Case-by-Case Approach

Throughout the amnesty debate, case-by-case review has often been proposed as a means of tailoring the relief offered each individual to the merits of his case. The Ford program applied individual review to each case, and the 1976 Democratic party platform and other amnesty proposals have suggested that this method be applied to military cases. This kind of review is often necessary to make sure that relief is not indiscriminately granted to people who do not deserve it. But its disadvantages are so great that it should only be used when it serves important policy purposes.

Without elaborate procedural safeguards, case-by-case review can be arbitrary, biased, and violative of due process. In the Ford program, the Justice and Defense Departments made case-by-case assignments of alternative service without setting careful standards to control their exercise of discretion. In doing so, they drew heavy criticism for the inconsistency of their decisions. A lawsuit raising due-process objections to the Defense Department program was still pending in late 1976.

Conversely, when procedural safeguards are fully implemented, a case-by-case process is extremely time-consuming and expensive. The military discharge review boards have recently been able to review only about 7,000 cases per year. President Ford's Clemency Board reviewed over 14,000 cases in six months of high-pressure activity. Statistics have shown its decisions to be fair, consistent, and nondiscriminatory. However, its procedures required 18 board members, a legal staff of 400, and an administrative staff of 200. Altogether, the board's decision-making cost about $10 million, or about $700 per case. Sitting in panels, each of which had to decide over 100 cases per day, the board spent less than five minutes discussing the typical case.*

---

*The Defense Department's Joint Alternative Service Board had an equally rapid process, without as much preparatory staff work as the Clemency Board.

Were a new program to review 100,000 cases on the Clemency
Board model, it would require an agency about the size of the
Federal Trade Commission to work for twelve to eighteen months
at a cost of around $50,000,000. Were it to review all 250,000
military cases one by one, an agency almost as large as the Justice
Department would be needed to complete the task in a reasonable
time.

A commitment of resources on this scale would be difficult to
justify. In most cases, individual review would make no real difference in the relief offered, and the files are not complete enough to
make fair decisions possible. The Ford clemency program justified
its case-by-case concept on the need to make fair alternative service assignments, a consideration which would not be relevant in a
program which imposed no such condition. Moreover, many of
the purposes of individual review can be accomplished by extending relief to carefully defined categories of cases. A clerical staff
can then apply objective criteria to make the necessary distinctions among cases through a rapid review of case files.

A case-by-case process is justified only in the following three
areas: (1) establishing the eligibility for borderline cases; (2)
screening categories which include a substantial number of people
who committed very serious offenses and who should be denied
relief; and (3) making veterans' benefits determinations for military offenders whose qualifications cannot be known without a
review of case files.

(1) Individual review should be applied to a few categories to
establish basic eligibility for the program. All cases involving offenses before or after the designated 1964–73 period, acts of civil
disobedience, and tax offenses must be reviewed to determine
whether these offenses were nonviolent and reasonably related
to the Vietnam War. Military cases involving court-martial discharges must be screened to assess whether the discharge resulted
from a distinctly military offense against discipline rather than a
civilian-type crime like robbery or assault. Also, all cases involving serious felony crimes must be disqualified from the program.
Perhaps 100,000 cases would have to be screened for these factors, but 95 percent or more would simply require a clerical review of the case file based upon objective criteria designated by
the presidential task force. Inescapably, a few thousand would
be borderline cases, requiring a measure of discretion. But even
in these cases, a comprehensive review of the entire record would

not be necessary. The inquiry should be directed just to the facts at issue and not the overall merit of an individual's case. Most cases involving borderline eligibility could be reviewed very quickly.

(2) A complete review of the case file is sometimes necessary to determine those Vietnam-era offenses so serious that they deserve no relief. This is a much more subjective process, requiring considerable procedural safeguards to assure that each decision is fairly made.

No category of draft offender warrants individual review. These offenses were not very diverse, and most case files would be incomplete, outdated, or nonexistent. For example, any case-by-case determinations involving fugitive draft offenders and nonregistrants would hinge entirely on unproven allegations by draft boards, prosecutors, or the offenders themselves. The files would be more complete for convicted draft offenders, but case-by-case review would hardly be worth the trouble. President Ford's Clemency Board found that only 0.3 percent of them committed draft offenses so serious that they did not deserve pardons.*

Military offenders are much more diverse, making a case-by-case approach necessary in some instances. Yet the number of truly bad cases is much smaller than most people realize, and they can be culled out without having to review all 250,000 military cases.

The largest category of military offenders—the over 200,000 who received administrative undesirable discharges—should be treated as a class. An undesirable discharge is not a criminal sanction, and the military's decision should be interpreted as a reliable judgment on the relative lack of seriousness of the misconduct. Furthermore, case records of former servicemen with undesirable discharges generally contain bare allegations without supporting evidence and without much description of the circumstances of the offense. No case-by-case determinations could fairly be based on these files alone.

The most serious military offenses were punished more severely by the military, and their case files include extensive investigative and trial records. The individual who refused to report to

*The Clemency Board denied clemency to 1 percent of its civilian applicants, usually becuase of other felony crimes not the seriousness of the draft offense itself.

Vietnam or fled from the combat zone was characteristically tried by court-martial for desertion, shirking hazardous duty, or comparable offenses. Servicemen who were convicted for these offenses should not be summarily denied relief, since many suffered from postcombat fatigue, were sincere conscientious objectors, or had other extenuating reasons for their offenses. Instead, all general court-martial cases and Vietnam-related special court-martial cases should be given careful individual review, with relief denied all those whose behavior cannot be condoned.* This would require approximately 20,000 case-by-case determinations.

(3) Veterans' benefits determinations generally require an assessment of a serviceman's entire record. However, a case-by-case review need not be applied to three-quarters of the former servicemen who would be issued general discharges under this program. Veterans who served satisfactory tours in Vietnam and persons with service-connected injuries merit automatic veterans' benefits.** Likewise, military offenders who did not serve two years in the armed forces should be automatically denied veterans' benefits under this program.*** Anyone who served two years or more in the armed forces should have his complete military file reviewed, upon his application to the Veterans Administration, to determine whether his military record warrants veterans' benefits. About 25,000 applications to the Veterans Administration could be expected over a period of several years.****

> *Recommendation 19:*
> All individuals should be granted or denied relief according to designated categories, except a case-by-case process should be used (1) to determine eligibility in borderline cases; (2) to screen categories which include a substantial

*For the specific categories of cases meriting case-by-case review, see pages

**Those with service-connected injuries who did not serve in Vietnam should only get medical benefits to cover those injuries. See pages 59–61.

***They still could apply for veterans' benefits, but their cases would be reviewed according to the standard criteria. To make this kind of distinction possible, new legislation would have to grant authority for a special kind of general discharge. See pages 59–61.

****About 50,000 servicemen would be covered by this standard, but the recent experience of Vietnam veterans suggests that about half would never apply for benefits.

number of people who committed very serious offenses; and (3) to make veterans' benefits determinations for persons with extended periods of military service.

Application of the Case-by-Case Approach

Leaving aside the veterans' benefits cases, the cases recommended for individual review number 20,000. They would have to be identified through a clerical review of official files, after which decisions could be made by an adjudicative body according to procedural and substantive standards set by the presidential task force. An effort should be made to contact each individual to invite him to submit a statement, clarify facts, and review an internally prepared summary of his case. However, one-third to one-half of the individuals would be unreachable, and those contacted would be unlikely to participate in the process in a substantial way. At the Clemency Board, very few people did more than just write a letter expalining their side of the case. Only 1 percent hired lawyers to represent them, and fewer than that requested personal appearances. Consequently, the case-by-case procedures would have to be administered to meet the special problems of an *ex parte* process.

The case-by-case review ordinarily should confine itself to those facts which triggered individual treatment in the first place. For eligibility determinations, the inquiry should focus only on the issues at hand: antiwar motivation, the nonviolent or distinctly military nature of a qualifying offense, or the seriousness of a felony crime. In the more comprehensive review of court-martial cases, the inquiry should be more extensive. Still, it should be confined to an examination of only those facts which bear on the individual's court-martialed offenses. However, the veterans' benefits determination should be very comprehensive, based upon a careful review of the individual's entire military record.

Recommendation 20:
Case-by-case procedures should ensure due process and fair treatment. The scope of review should be confined to facts relevant to the specific question at hand.

Categories of Individuals

To be effective and fair, a program must be tailored to the needs and merits of widely differing types of cases. This does not require case-by-case review in all instances, but it does mean that each category of offenders must be treated differently. Inescapably, this adds to the complexity of a program, but the diversity of these categories does not lend itself to a simplified, unitary approach.

There are thirteen separate categories of civilian and military offenders who could be included. They are listed below, and each is discussed in turn.

Draft Offenders

*1. Fugitive draft offenders (3,000)
 2. American expatriates who acquire foreign citizenship (5,000)
*3. Individuals who never registered for the draft (250,000)
*4. Convicted draft offenders (8,800)
 5. Individuals convicted for destroying their draft cards (33)

Other Civilian Offenders

6. Individuals convicted for acts of civil disobedience motivated by opposition to the Vietnam War (number unknown)
7. Individuals convicted for refusing to pay taxes as a consequence of the Vietnam War (10)
8. Individuals convicted for state and local offenses motivated by opposition to the Vietnam War (number unknown)

Military Offenders

 *9. Fugitive military offenders (3,000)
*10. Military offenders with undesirable discharges, bad-conduct discharges, or dishonorable discharges for absence offenses (100,000)
 11. Military offenders with undesirable, bad-conduct, or dishonorable discharges for nonabsence offenses (150,000)
 12. Former servicemen with general discharges (300,000)

Miscellaneous

*13. Applicants to President Ford' clemency program (21,800)

*Eligible for President Ford's clemency program.

Fugitive Draft Offenders (3,000)

Throughout the entire Vietnam period, perhaps 25,000 draft offenders took exile, 20,000 of whom went to Canada. Most eventually returned to the United States, and there are now only about 3,000 exiles who still face draft charges.*

From the start, many exiles looked upon themselves as expatriates and Canadian immigrants. The adjustment was not always easy, and jobs were often scarce. The Canadian social welfare programs helped them to survive their most difficult periods, but life as an immigrant was hard enough to prompt thousands to return home and take their chances with the courts. Those who remained in Canada eventually settled into careers and life-styles similar to what they would have had back home.

As a group, the draft exiles defy generalization. No reliable statistics are available to indicate their background, but they appear to be a true cross-section of American youth. They are blacks and whites, from every type of family background, spanning all levels of educational achievement. Some left because of a deeply felt moral opposition to the war. A good many others left because they saw no alternative to their personal difficulties with the draft. Some refused to cooperate with the draft as a matter of principle, but most were too frightened, impatient, confused, or ill informed to take advantage of the system's many loopholes. Relatively few fled as the last step in a well-orchestrated campaign to avoid the draft.

Most of the 3,000 who remain in exile have undergone an irreversible change in their lives. They have careers, families, and permanent homes. Their inability to visit the United States is still a hardship to them and their families. But that hardship is far outweighed by the fear of prosecution and imprisonment, so few are willing to come home and have their cases tested in the courts. Even if the Justice Department were to dismiss the charges against them, the overwhelming majority would probably continue to live in Canada.

By contrast, nearly all of the 210,000 individuals cited for apparent draft violations stayed home to face the charges. Some

---

*Five thousand expatriates are barred from reentering the United States, almost all of whom have had their draft charges dropped. Other one-time draft fugitives are still living in Canada even though they are free to return to the United States. See pages 78–80.

entered the service as an alternative to prosecution, and others had their charges dropped when they failed their physical examinations. A survey of federal prosecutors indicated that over half—about 115,000—went free because defective draft board procedures made their induction orders unenforceable. In some districts, prosecutors rejected 80–90 percent of their cases for this reason. Just 8,800 people were convicted.*

Beginning in the mid-1960s and accelerating thereafter, Selective Service cases became increasingly difficult to prosecute successfully. The Selective Service System was faced with widespread legal challenges to its procedures, and many induction orders were deemed illegal and unenforceable by federal judges. Local draft boards found themselves bound by administrative requirements they were ill equipped to satisfy. Draft officials were often unsympathetic and unresponsive to due process standards imposed by judges. As a consequence, many individuals were cited by Selective Service for violations that did not withstand legal scrutiny.

As courts dismissed thousands of cases for procedural irregularities of increasing complexity and detail, federal prosecutors became correspondingly strict in the standards they imposed on cases referred by draft boards. In 1970 a series of Supreme Court decisions undermined the prosecutors' ability to convict most of their remaining cases. Thousands of inactive cases were dropped. Many others remained inactive awaiting only the eventual surrender of fugitives before these too would be dropped.

By late 1974, the Justice Department showed little enthusiasm for prosecuting unresolved draft cases. The announcement of the Ford clemency program disclosed the existence of large numbers of unprocessed cases in U.S. attorneys' offices. Under Congressional pressure, the Justice Department conducted a fast review of these cases. Of a stated number of 6,200 active cases and approximately 11,000 inactive cases, it dismissed all but 4,522 as being of no prosecutorial merit. In January, 1975, the Justice Department announced that no draft violators, except for nonregistrants, would be prosecuted if their names were not on this final Kennedy list. This amounted to

*See pages 83–85.

granting unconditional amnesty to about 8,000 individuals.*

Since the conclusion of the Ford clemency program, the number of outstanding prosecutions has continued to fall. Of the original 4,522 on the Kennedy list, about 600 accepted the clemency offer, 400 of whom have faithfully done alternative service.** Another 230 draft offenders have been convicted and 30 acquitted after trial. An additional 411 have had their indictments formally dismissed. A good many others, perhaps 500, have had their cases quietly dropped by federal prosecutors in the pre-indictment stage. There has been no official survey of the Kennedy list since its original publication in January 1975, so the number of individuals still facing prosecution cannot be accurately determined. The Justice Department reports that there are 2,677 indictments still outstanding, not counting an untallied number of other cases under active investigation. Thus at present, one can estimate that about 3,000 individuals are still subject to prosecution.*** Some of the cases are pending only because U.S. attorneys and judges often refuse to dismiss them without the personal presence of the defendant.

If the Justice Department were to review all outstanding cases according to consistent, up-to-date legal requirements, many would be dropped. Yet even those which could be successfully prosecuted would probably not involve prison sentences. Recent sentences for draft offenders have been very lenient, with only 9 percent given prison terms in fiscal 1975.

However, it is unlikely that more than a handful of the 3,000 fugitives still in exile face actual prosecution. Few would suffer punishment if they came home, but only the most homesick are willing to take that chance. No interest is served by continuing to single out those individuals. With 8,000 former fugitives granted "amnesty" by the publication of the Kennedy list, and with tens of thousands of draft cases dropped through-

*Five thousand others were not "amnestied" since they had accepted foreign citizenship and could be barred from the United States as aliens. See pages 34–37.

**Approximately 100 others, who were nonregistrants, also took advantage of the program.

***This number cannot be computed from the other figures because some of the convicted, acquitted, and dismissed cases involve people who signed up for clemency.

out the Vietnam era, there is no reason not to do the same for
the 3,000 who remain vulnerable.

There is no need to grant them pardons; simply dropping unindicted cases and dismissing indicted cases would be sufficient.*
Some also face charges of bail-jumping or illegal flight, emanat-
ing from their original draft offenses. These charges should also
be dropped.

> *Recommendation 21:*
> All charges against fugitive draft offenders should be dis-
> missed. No pardons are necessary.

American Expatriates Who Acquired Foreign Citizenship (5,000)

Most draft exiles who went to Canada did so in the early years
of the war, between 1966 and 1969. They usually obtained
landed immigrant status quickly. Five years later, between 1971
and 1974, they qualified for Canadian citizenship. Many intended
to remain permanently in Canada and eagerly accepted its citizenship. Others were more ambivalent about the future. They
wanted to keep their American ties; yet they feared that they
could never come home without facing prosecution. Reluctantly,
they accepted Canadian citizenship as the best way to cope with
an uncertain future.

The acceptance of foreign citizenship was much more widespread among draft offenders than military offenders. Military
exiles rarely arrived in Canada until 1968, and many lived for
months or years in the underground before becoming landed immigrants. As a result, very few completed the five-year waiting
period before 1975. Likewise, the exodus to Sweden began in
1968, and only a handful were able to bypass Sweden's usual
seven-year waiting period and become citizens before 1975.

By 1975, three important events had occurred. First, President Ford's clemency program regarded these expatriates as
"aliens" and excluded them from relief. Second, the Justice Department published the Kennedy list, informing many fugitives
for the first time that the American government did not intend
to prosecute them. Third, the Justice Department's Immigration

---

*Pardons for unconvicted individuals involve an inference of legal guilt,
making them inapplicable to cases which appear to be of questionable
prosecutorial merit. See pages 52–56.

and Naturalization Service made it clear that all expatriates who fled the country to avoid military service would be barred from reentering the United States, whether or not they had been convicted or were still subject to prosecution. As a result, those who accepted foreign citizenship discovered that they faced permanent exclusion from the United States. With these facts in mind, few exiles have accepted foreign citizenship during the past two years. Today, about 5,000 American expatriates face permanent exclusion from the United States.

A small number of these individuals were convicted of draft violations before they left for Canada. Most of the rest of these individuals had their cases dropped in the years before 1974 or when their names were left off the Kennedy list.*

Expatriates who wish to reassert their American citizenship must make application to the Immigration and Naturalization Service, which reviews each case on its facts to determine whether each individual voluntarily renounced American citizenship. Sometimes this renunciation was overt, and sometimes it can only be inferred from the acceptance of foreign citizenship. Those who merely wish to visit the United States are often fearful of undergoing formal hearings, lest they be barred by an exclusion order which can be difficult to remove. In emergencies, they can pay a fee and receive a special waiver allowing them only to travel directly to and from a stated destination.

As a group, these expatriates are fundamentally no different from other draft fugitives. Their acceptance of foreign citizenship or renunciation of American citizenship often resulted from the failure of the Justice Department and Selective Service to keep them informed about the status of their prosecutions. They should not be punished for an oversight of the federal government. They should be able to reenter the United States freely, and they should be offered the chance to regain their American citizenship rights if they wish.

Similar problems are faced by several one-time immigrants to the United States who returned to their native countries or went into exile during the war. They were subject to the draft under the terms of their residence in the United States. Almost all have

*"Aliens" were not eligible for the Ford program. Accordingly, many prosecutors omitted expatriates from the names they submitted to the Justice Department. Prosecution was thereby precluded.

roots in their native countries, but some came to the United
States as children or teenagers and consider America their true
home. Once these young men left the country, they were excluded from reentry. Some have been separated from families
who remained in the United States. These individuals should
also be accorded relief.

Reentry rights can be granted administratively through a
change of Justice Department policy. The statutory provision
barring reentry could be interpreted to apply only to those with
unpardoned draft or military convictions, or still subject to prosecution for draft or military offenses. If this policy change were
accompanied by the rest of the recommended program, no Vietnam-era offenders would thereafter be barred from reentering
the United States.

Restoring citizenship rights can be done administratively only
through awkward case-by-case determinations that these individuals did not renounce American citizenship voluntarily. For
some, this would require an interpretation that any act induced
by fear of prosecution was "involuntary." However, this would
be a strained and artificial interpretation of existing standards.
A much better remedy would be to seek legislative authority to
treat Vietnam-era offenders as a special class for the purpose of
reestablishing their earlier rights of citizenship.

> *Recommendation 22:*
> American expatriates and other foreign citizens who left
> the United States to avoid military service should be per-
> mitted to visit the United States.

> *Recommendation 23:*
> Individuals who lost American citizenship because of
> the Vietnam War should be able to restore their rights
> taking the standard oath of citizenship. (This requires
> new legislation.)

Individuals Who Never Registered for the Draft (250,000)

Despite the earlier termination of induction authority, men
were required until 1975 to register for the draft within a few
days of their eighteenth birthday. Those who never registered
faced prosecution and imprisonment upon discovery, and there
were few legal defenses that could be raised in their behalf.

Throughout the Vietnam era, only about 250 people were convicted for failing to register for the draft. Many more were identified, but allowed to register late and escape prosecution. Some federal prosecutors continued this lenient policy even for nonregistrants who waited until the draft was over before surrendering.

Estimates of the number of nonregistrants vary widely. Some have compared registration data with census data, concluding that as many as 2 million people never registered. But census figures cannot be used to measure nonregistrants. The census itself has about a 3 percent error rate, which probably exceeds the number of nonregistrants, and many of those who never registered are the same people who are never counted by the census. A survey of 1,586 draft-eligible men in South Bend, Indiana, Ann Arbor, Michigan, and Washington, D.C., discovered twenty-one nonregistrants, the largest number in Washington, D.C. Extrapolating from these findings, it appears that a more accurate estimate of Vietnam-era nonregistrants is 250,000,* almost half of whom are black.

Most nonregistrants were youths from disadvantaged backgrounds—especially inner-city youths, itinerants, and migrant laborers. For many, nonregistration simply reflected their nonparticipation in the American mainstream. Sometimes, young people were so ill informed that they never realized that they had to register for the draft. Even if they were aware of what was expected of the, underprivileged youths had so few of the benefits of citizenship that they felt no need to assume any of its obligations. The Vietnam War may have had a significant impact on nonregistration offenses among blacks. In contrast to white nonregistrants, almost all black nonregistrants committed their offenses in the latter years of the war. Apparently, rising opposition to the war within the black community made blacks reluctant to join the military. Nonregistration was an obvious way to avoid the draft.

Their white, middle-calss counterparts saw nonregistration as a much more dangerous means of draft avoidance. Draft boards sometimes checked high school yearbooks to make sure that all

---

*The survey sample was not representative of American youth as a whole, and its spot-sampling methodology made it not perfectly representative of the three locations surveyed. Therefore, the 250,000 figure has a substantial error factor. The exact number of nonregistrants is probably between 150,000 and 350,000.

graduating seniors had registered on time. By the early 1970s the antiwar movement spread to the high schools, and seventeen-year-olds were sometimes encouraged to resist the draft by not registering. Some antiwar counselors circulated pamphlets encouraging nonregistration as the safest means of draft avoidance. They were probably right—only 0.1 percent of all nonregistrants were ever convicted—but the data do not indicate any surge in white nonregistration offenses late in the war.

Today, nonregistrants are safer than ever before. Draft boards no longer exist, police almost never ask to see draft cards, and neighbors are much less suspicious. Even those who are discovered are unlikely to be prosecuted successfully. In the 1971 *Toussie* case, the Supreme Court interpreted the draft law prior to 1970 as barring prosecutions for nonregistration after an individual turned twenty three.* Following this decision, the Congress changed the law in September 1971 to enable nonregistrants to be prosecuted until they turned thirty one. But the recent *Dickerson* case in the Third Circuit held that nonregistrants who turned eighteen before the 1971 change in the law had to be prosecuted, if ever, before they turned twenty three. They all are now over twenty three and safe, if other courts follow the *Dickerson* rule. No nonregistrant has been convicted since *Dickerson*, and most federal prosecutors are uncertain whether that rule would be applied in their circuits. In addition, federal prosecutors rarely press charges against nonregistrants who would not have been drafted. Since draft calls for nineteen-year-olds ended in December 1972, only those nonregistrants who turned eighteen between September 1971 and December 1971 still face a realistic threat of prosecution.

With nonregistrants unlikely to be discovered and with *Dickerson* indicating that few of them still face prosecution, the issue seems to be moot. There is little point in continuing to subject 250,000 men to the remote risk of five years in prison.

> *Recommendation 24:*
> Nonregistration cases should no longer be prosecuted.

*The statute of limitations was—and still is—five years. Before 1971, a nonregistration offense was considered to occur only once, five days after an individual's eighteenth birthday. After 1971, it was considered a continuing offense, lasting until an individual's draft vulnerability expired on his twenty-sixth birthday.

Convicted Draft Offenders (8,800)

Of the 210,000 accused persons cited for Selective Service Act violations by their draft boards and referred to the Justice Department between 1964 and 1973, 25,000 were indicted, 10,000 tried, and only 8,800 convicted. In other areas of the criminal law, usually 30 to 40 percent of all known offenders are convicted.

Unlike draft-card burners, they were not convicted through a conscious policy of selective prosecution, nor were their offenses especially serious. Less than 1 percent were convicted because of fraudulent draft evasion, and President Ford's Clemency Board found only 15 percent to have engaged in "selfish and manipulative" behavior. For the most part, they were unwilling or unable to avail themselves of the many avenues for escape which existed throughout the draft system. Instead, they failed to register for the draft, keep their draft boards informed of their whereabouts, report for preinduction physical examinations, report for or submit to induction, or do alternative service as conscientious objectors.

Three-fourths of all convicted draft offenders were opposed to the war in one respect or another. Many refused, on principle, to cooperate in any way with the draft. They rejected available deferment and exemptions and refused to raise technical defense at trial. Some insisted on challenging the fundamental legality of the Vietnam War, and other wanted to bear witness to what they considered unconscionable war policies by submitting themselves to conviction and imprisonment.

Many others were conscientiously opposed to the war, but were unable to qualify for the draft exemptions they thought they deserved. About 25 percent were Jehovah's Witnesses or Muslims whose beliefs did not conform with Selective Service requirements. Jehovah's Witnesses considered themselves ministers, but the law considered them conscientious objectors subject to alternative service. Their faith barred them from obeying alternative service orders given by Selective Service and they were often prosecuted for this failure. Muslims refused to submit to induction because the Vietnam War was not sanctioned by Allah. Since their faith did not preclude participation in all wars, they did not qualify for CO status and were convicted when they refused induction. Other pacifists had their conscientious-objector applications rejected because they were not based on religious beliefs. Many were convicted before the Supreme Court changed this rule. Despite the courts' retroactive application of these deicsions, the Justice Department took no steps to have past convictions overturned. A good many others were convicted even after the court decisions because of ill-informed lawyers and judges.

About one-fourth of the convicted draft offenders were young men from disadvantaged backgrounds who did not fully understand their draft obligations. Typically, they led itinerant lives and did not receive communications from their draft boards.* Some had physical or mental disqualifications which would have kept them out of military service, but they were nonetheless convicted for draft offenses. In some instances, the draft law was used to suppress civil rights activities. In Mississippi and Louisiana, several black activists experienced hurried-up induction orders, prosecution, and long terms of imprisonment.

Less than half of all convicted offenders went to prison, and most of those served six months or less in confinement. Sentences varied greatly among different regions of the country and from year to year. In fiscal year 1967, 89 percent of all convicted draft offenders were sentenced to prison; by fiscal year 1974, just 9 percent were sentenced to prison, and many were given very short terms of probation.

Just a few persons are still in prison for draft convictions. A larger number, perhaps several hundred, are now on probation or parole, with reporting requirements and other restraints on their freedom. For the most part, convicted draft offenders are no longer subject to active legal restraints. However, they continue to suffer legal disabilities and the social stigma of a felony criminal record.

Recommendation 25:
Individuals convicted of draft offenses should be issued pardons.

---

*Every draft registrant was required by law to make sure that communications from his draft board could always reach him. Failure to receive an induction order was not a valid defense to a draft charge.

Individuals Convicted for Destroying Their Draft Cards (33)

Early in the Vietnam War, opposition to the war and draft resistance were often expressed by burning or mutilating draft cards in a public ceremony. Congress responded in 1965 by making this a felony punishable by up to five years in prison. In the next few years, thousands of draft registrants challenged the new law.

To counter this open defiance, the Justice Department pursued a conscious policy of selective prosecution. Of the many thousands who openly destroyed their cards, forty six were prosecuted, and thirty three were convicted. Almost always, they were sentenced to long prison terms. When their convictions were upheld by the Supreme Court in the 1968 *O'Brien* case, draft-card burnings became much less frequent.

The destruction of one's draft card cannot be fairly distinguished from other draft offenses, so relief should be afforded here as well. Burning or mutilating a draft card was a personal response to the draft, very much like the act of publicly refusing to submit to induction. Unlike the wholesale mutilation of irreplaceable Selective Service records, no significant destruction of federal property was involved and the operation of the draft was not impaired. A draft board could order an individual to report for induction whether or not he possessed his draft card.

Above all, these were acts of a political and symbolic nature, which despite *O'Brien,* should be regarded as a legitimate exercise of freedom of speech. Many legal scholars consider *O'Brien* to have been wrongly decided in light of several Vietnam-era Supreme Court cases upholding other forms of dissent, like defacing the flag, which were no less provocative.

> *Recommendation 26:*
> Individuals convicted of destroying their draft cards should be issued pardons.

Individuals Convicted for Acts of Civil Disobedience Motivated by Opposition to the Vietnam War (number unknown)

Throughout the Vietnam War, individuals engaged in various forms of protest which did not involve personal draft vulnerability. Men and women of all ages participated in these anti-protests, many of which resulted in arrests on federal charges. Most arrests involved temporary obstruction of government activities, trespass, or other nonviolent activities, usually as a result of sit-ins. However, not all these arrests resulted in convictions; and many convictions were later overturned on constitutional or other grounds. Nonetheless, an undetermined number of people have federal misdemeanor or felony conviction records as a consequence of antiwar demonstrations.

These individuals were generally motivated by strong antiwar beliefs, and many conscientiously chose to break the law as a form of protest. Accordingly, they should be encompassed in a program which offers relief to individuals who committed other violations in connection with the war.

However, a distinction must be drawn between nonviolent and violent forms of protest. Antiwar radicals engaged in several attacks on draft boards, induction stations, and other government facilities which resulted in the destruction of records and other property. Regardless of one's sincerity or the worth of one's cause, the use of force or the destruction of property cannot be condoned and should not be relieved of the full penalty of the law.

Before and after the Vietnam era, many people have engaged in similar forms of civil disobedience to demonstrate their support for civil rights and other causes. Whether these individuals should also be pardoned need not be addressed in a Vietnam-oriented program. Therefore, civil disobedience cases should be reviewed individually to establish eligibility. Pardons should be granted to those whose offenses were nonviolent and apparently motivated by opposition to the Vietnam War. Despite the hazards of applying such a test of conscience it cannot be avoided without expanding the program far beyond its basic relationship to the Vietnam War.*

> *Recommendation 27:*
> Individuals convicted of federal offenses for acts of civil disobedience related to the Vietnam War should be issued pardons if their offenses were (1) nonviolent, and (2) motivated by opposition to the Vietnam War.

*See pages 67–69.

Individuals Convicted for Refusing to Pay Taxes as a Consequence of the Vietnam War (10)

The Vietnam War imposed two direct obligations on American citizens—serving in the military and paying taxes to support the war. In the late 1960s, some antiwar groups seized upon federal income taxes and telephone taxes as a means of expressing their opposition to the Vietnam War. Usually, the Internal Revenue Service responded by attaching assets and wages to force payment. However, some people listed Vietnamese as dependents or made similar improper claims on their tax forms. They openly admitted what they were doing but were prosecuted for tax fraud. In all, about ten people were convicted for tax violations of this kind, and most were sentenced to prison. They also had to pay their taxes.

Like those who deliberately violated the draft law as a means of expressing their opposition to the war, these were conscientiously motivated people who engaged in a nonviolent form of civil disobedience. Yet unlike draft offenders, they had to fulfill their legal obligations in addition to paying a penalty under the criminal law. As such they merit relief under a post-Vietnam program.

These ten cases would be very difficult to identify clerically among the thousands of tax convictions during the period which bore no relationship to the war. Instead, they should be informed of their eligibility for relief through the public information program. Upon their personal application, their cases should be reviewed individually to establish eligibility.* To protect the integrity of the tax law, pardons should be granted only to those who can clearly demonstrate that their offenses were motivated by opposition to the Vietnam War.

> *Recommendation 28:*
> Individuals convicted of federal tax offenses should be issued pardons if their offenses were motivated by opposition to the Vietnam War.

Individuals Convicted for State and Local Offenses Motivated by Opposition to the Vietnam War (number unknown)

Most arrests and convictions arising out of antiwar demonstrations involved violations of state laws and municipal ordinances. These convictions were almost always for misdemeanors or lesser violations for which people rarely were sent to jail. Like federal offenders, however, these individuals have criminal records.

*See pages 63–65 and 69–73.

Because these are state and local matters, they are not the proper subject of action by the president or Congress. However the president should urge state and local authorities to grant relief consistent with the overall scope of his post-Vietnam program. In addition, the president should order the Civil Service Commission and other federal agencies to disregard state convictions for antiwar demonstrations when considering applications for federal employment. This could be done by amending federal job application forms to enable Vietnam-era offenders to avoid having to list convictions for any nonviolent offenses arising out of antiwar activities.

> *Recommendation 29:*
> State and local governments should be encouraged to offer relief to individuals convicted of nonviolent offenses motivated by opposition to the Vietnam War.

> *Recommendation 30:*
> Individuals applying for federal employment should not be required to list convictions for nonviolent state and local offenses motivated by opposition to the Vietnam War.

Fugitive Military Offenders (3,000)

Throughout the Vietnam War, soldiers went AWOL no more frequently than their counterparts in the Korean War. What was unique about the Vietnam-era was the number of long-term absences. After thirty days, an unauthorized absnece was administratively considered a desertion offense, and the Vietnam-era incidence of desertion was three times that of the Korean War.

Only about 15 percent of the absence offenders were directly motivated by their opposition to the Vietnam War.* A much greater percentage faced personal and family problems or else could not adjust to military service. One-fourth were blacks or members of other minority groups. Over half came from broken homes, often with poverty-level incomes. They typically grew up in small towns or farms, and a disproportionate number came from the South. Often they were individuals who had trouble in civilian life. Most were high school dropouts who had volunteered

---

*Various official and unofficial studies have produced figures ranging from 4 percent to 30 percent. See the footnote on page 7.

for the service. In the military, their inability to cope resulted in absence offenses.

Few of them became true "fugitives." Nine out of ten either surrendered quickly or resumed a normal life under their own names, usually in their hometowns. Their absence offenses often lasted for years, despite the military's notification to local police. Several thousand moved around the United States under assumed names, often hiding in college communities or traveling through the antiwar underground which spanned the nation. Others took exile. In the early years of the Vietnam War, no foreign country accepted foreign deserters. Those who slipped across Canadian or Mexican borders were usually delivered to American military police when they were discovered. In early 1968, the first opportunity arose for military fugitives to settle in another country when Sweden announced that it would accept them as political refugees. Shortly afterwards, Canada adopted the same attitude, and soldiers increasingly chose Canada or Sweden over life in the American underground. Throughout the war years, about 15,000 fugitive soldiers took exile; 10,000 went to Canada, 1,000 went to Sweden, and the rest scattered around the world.

Life in exile was difficult, especially in foreign countries which threatened to deport fugitives upon discovery. Even in Canada or Sweden, jobs were hard to find for these young Americans, most of whom were poorly educated and had no job skills. By the early 1970s, many began coming home to face military punishment.

Starting in 1971, the military began to offer administrative undesirable discharges in unprecedented numbers to surrendering absence offenders who did not insist upon standing trial. Most were eager to end their military status as quickly as possible, especially if they could avoid the risk of months or years in military prison. But those who returned from Canada or Sweden with outspoken antiwar views were usually denied this opportunity; most were court-martialed and sentenced to long prison terms. Thereafter, military offenders who returned from exile paid their own passage back to the United States, concealed where they had been, and received immediate undesirable discharges.

In the last few years, the military has trimmed its backlog of fugitive cases significantly. In the early 1970s, the military believed that as many as 30,000 absence offenders were still at large. By the start of the Ford clemency program, that number had been reduced to 10,000. Today, there are only about 3,000

Vietnam-era military fugitives, most of whom are probably in
Canada or Sweden.

As a result of the Ford program, all branches of service now
consistently offer administrative undesirable discharges to returning absence offenders. The only cases now being referred to
court-martial are those involving serious civilian-type offenses
against person or property. About 10 percent of those who surrender are given general discharges because of extenuating circumstances surrounding their cases. Unlike earlier years, politically motivated exiles are not treated more harshly.

With the military having adopted a policy of leniency for
fugitive absence offenders, a new program should not attempt
to distinguish among them. They should be treated as a class.
The only exception should be for those who also face charges
for civilian-type offenses which warrant trial by general court-
martial. Their cases should be identified by a clerical review of
the files, and those who the military believes can be successfully prosecuted should be excluded from the program.

The most important relief which can be offered fugitive military offenders is their immediate separation from the service.
Many are still unaware that under present policy they can be
discharged without having to face court-martial. As a group,
their offenses were no different from those of offenders who
have already been discharged, so their relief should also be
no different. It should include general discharges plus
benefits if they qualify under the standards established by
this program.

> *Recommendation 31:*
> Fugitive military offenders should be issued general
> discharges *in absentia,* except those charged with ci-
> vilian-type offenses which warrant trial by general
> court-martial.

*Military Offenders with Undesirable, Bad-Conduct, or
Dishonorable Discharges for Absence Offenses (100,000)*

About 100,000 of the 250,000 Vietnam-era former servicemen with bad discharges* were discharged for one of three

---

*From Fiscal Year 1965 through Fiscal Year 1974, approximately
235,000 servicemen were given bad discharges. (Fiscal Year 1974 must
be included in this tally because most offenders would have been draftees

absence offenses: unauthorized absence, missing movement, or desertion.* About three-fourths were given undesirable discharges administratively and were separated without further military punishment. The other one-fourth were court-martialed, given bad-conduct or dishonorable discharges, and usually sentenced to a few months in military prison.**

Of the 100,000 former servicemen with bad discharges for absence offenses, a very small percentage committed acts that were demonstrably cowardly or which endangered the lives of fellow troops. Throughout the entire war, just twenty-four soldiers were convicted of desertion under combat conditions. Only about 12,000 committed absence offenses in Vietnam or upon receiving orders for Vietnam.*** By contrast, 20,000 fled after completing one or more full Vietnam tours, and the remaining 68,000 were discharged for absence offenses which bore no relationship to service in Vietnam.

In the early years of the war, absence offenses were generally punished by court-martial, imprisonment, and bad-conduct or dishonorable discharges. Paradoxically, what many would regard as the most serious absence offenses—failure to report to the combat zone and AWOL in Vietnam—did not receive unusually severe treatment by the military. In fact, a soldier who committed an absence offense wholly unrelated to Vietnam service was more likely to be discharged by court-martial than a soldier whose offense occurred in Vietnam.

Beginning in the early 1970s, the use of courts-martial fell precipitously. Instead, most absence offenders were given the opportunity of accepting an administrative undesirable discharge in lieu of trial. In part, the widespread use of administrative discharges reflected an acknowledgment by commanding officers

---

or draft-induced enlistees.) A few thousand others would be covered by this program because of earlier or later offenses related to the Vietnam War.

*In military law, "desertion" is unauthorized absence with an intent to remain away permanently, an intent to avoid hazardous duty, or other aggravating circumstances. Only 9 percent of all punished offenders were convicted of desertion.

**Of the 250,000 bad discharges, about 210,000 were undesirable discharges, one-third for absence offenses; 40,000 were bad-conduct or dishonorable discharges imposed by courts-martial, three-fourths for absence offenses.

***Seven thousand fled when ordered to Vietnam; 2,000 went AWOL in the combat zone; 2,000 went AWOL in a Vietnam noncombat zone; 1,000 failed to return to Vietnam from leave.

that most absence offenses did not warrant a criminal conviction and possible imprisonment.

In offering relief to military absence offenders, a new program should be generous with the overwhelming majority of cases, while excluding relief only to those who committed the most serious offenses without extenuating circumstances.

An exhaustive review of all 100,000 cases is not necessary to isolate the most serious absence offenses. Such an undertaking would require immense resources and could never be done fairly. It is impossible to make an *ex post facto* determination that a commanding officer was too lenient with an offender when he allowed him to avoid court-martial and accept an undesirable discharge. At the time, the commanding officer had the benefit of considerable evidence about motivation, contrition, the quality of military performance, and many other facts which were never put into official files. The military files of absence offenders with undesirable discharges describe little more than the time and place of the alleged offenses. Important facts are often omitted. Even the fact of the offense itself cannot be taken for granted; the administrative process was not a trial, and the soldier's acceptance of an undesirable discharge was not an admission of guilt. The military decision to proceed administratively offers reasonable grounds for categorizing the 70,000 absence offenders with undesirable discharges as having committed relatively less serious absence offenses. They should be given automatic relief, without undergoing a case-by-case review.

Because of the large amount of discretion exercised by commanders, discharge policies were often applied inconsistently. Not every court-martial necessarily reflected a more serious offense. Further distinctions must therefore be made among the 30,000 discharges awarded by courts-martial. Under military law a special court-martial may not impose a dishonorable discharge or a sentence involving confinement for more than six months. Special courts-martial are thus akin to misdemeanor courts in civilian law. For this reason, a decision to refer a case to a special court-martial reflects the commanding officer's view that the offenses charged are not of the most serious nature. Nevertheless, any absence offense related to service in Vietnam should be considered serious if it was punished by special court-martial, and these cases should be reviewed individually.

A general court-martial is convened only when the commanding officer believes that a felony offense has occurred. It is the only military court which may sentence an offender to a dishonorable discharge and more than six months in military prison. All general court-martial cases should therefore be reviewed individually, whether or not related to Vietnam service. Applying these standards, about 15,000 court-martial cases would undergo a case-by-case review to determine whether relief is warranted.

> *Recommendation 32:*
> Individuals discharged for absence offenses should be treated as follows:
> (1) Individuals with undesirable discharges should be issued general discharges;
> (2) a case-by-case review should determine whether pardons and general discharges should be issued to individuals discharged by general court-martial;
> (3) a case-by-case review should determine whether pardons and general discharges should be issued to individuals discharged by special court-martial for (a) absence in Vietnam, (b) failure to report to Vietnam, or (c) failure to return to Vietnam from leave;
> (4) other individuals discharged by special court-martial should be issued pardons and general discharges.

Military Offenders with Undesirable, Bad-Conduct, or Dishonorable Discharges for Nonabsence Offenses (150,000)

Throughout the amnesty debate, the focus of discussion has been on "deserters." Absence offenses have been wrongly associated with antiwar motivations, leading many people to ignore three basic facts. First, the great majority of absence offenders left their units because of personal or family problems, not because of their opposition to the war. Second, antiwar behavior was manifested in a great many kinds of offenses. Third, many absence offenders and nonabsence offenders exhibited common behavior patterns.

The Ford clemency program recognized the first point but not the other two. The program included all 100,000 discharged

absence offenders regardless of the individual's motivation, but
it excluded 150,000 servicemen with bad discharges for other
offenses, even those with very similar characteristics. This produced the following anomalies: If a soldier fled when he received orders for Vietnam, he was eligible for the program;
if he stood his ground and refused to obey those orders, he was
ineligible. If an offender committed a series of absence and nonabsence offenses, he was eligible for clemency only if his last
offense involved unauthorized absence; if it did not, he was
ineligible.*

Most former servicemen discharged for violations of military
discipline were not explicitly antiwar, but like absence offenders they were strongly affected by the war. Recruits reflected
the same antipathy toward authority as others in their generation. Even those who were not consciously antiwar were often
confused and upset by the public controversy about the war.
Racial conflict and drug problems were widespread. Commis-
sioned and noncommissioned officers at the company and platoon levels were frequently young and inexperienced, making
it difficult for them to maintain morale and cope with these
matters. As a result, the armed forces experienced a wide range
of disciplinary problems—disrespect, refusal to obey orders,
drug abuse, unauthorized absence, and other misconduct.

A bad discharge was often the product of a complex pattern
of substandard performance. It is not possible to make a precise distinction between persons discharged for absence and
those discharged for other violations of military discipline.
Some servicemen repeatedly went AWOL but were not discharged until they committed some other form of misconduct.
Others were discharged after a long history of nonabsence infractions followed by an otherwise insignificant AWOL. A military
record exhibiting a pattern of misconduct typically resulted in
a bad discharge for the latest act even if that violation standing
alone might have led to a lesser form of disciplinary action.

Commanding officers had broad discretion to decide how to
separate servicemen who had demonstrated an incapacity or

*The Ford program limited eligibility to servicemen discharged "as a
consequence" of unauthorized absence, but many of the cases reviewed
by the Clemency Board involved persons with both absence and nonabsence misconduct. Discharges were based on the entire military record, an
and attributing the separation to one cause was artificial.

unwillingness to perform well. Frequently, they responded to nonabsence offenses by giving offenders undesirable discharges following administrative determinations that they were "unfit" for military service. Military guidelines for "unfitness" discharges were very broad, encompassing drug usage, shirking duty, frequent trouble with civilian or military authority, failure to pay debts, and homosexuality.

Undesirable discharges for unfitness were especially common during the first several years of the Vietnam War. As the war neared its end, morale problems eased, and the military began to rely more on rehabilitation, counseling, and more lenient discharge policies. Many who once would have received undesirable discharges for "unfitness" instead were often given general discharges for "unsuitability." They were thereby spared a discharge under other than honorable conditions, and they became eligible for veterans' benefits.

The program should not make an artificial distinction between absence offenses and other violations of military discipline. Former servicemen who received bad discharges for nonabsence offenses against military discipline should be treated exactly the same as absence offenders. Thus, all nonabsence offenders granted undesirable discharges should be granted relief as a class.* Individuals discharged by a special court-martial for military offenses connected with Vietnam service should be reviewed on a case-by-case basis, as should all whose offenses resulted in discharge after a general court-martial. Applying these standards, about 5,000 court-martial cases would undergo a case-by-case review to determine whether relief is warranted.

However, some nonabsence offenses were civilian-type crimes and were not simply violations of military discipline. Several thousand soldiers were convicted by courts-martial, sentenced to prison, and given bad-conduct or dishonorable discharges for murder, rape, armed robbery, assault, theft, and other serious criminal misconduct. Former servicemen convicted by special or general court-martial or civilian-type offenses against person or property should be excluded altogether.**

---

*Many soldiers were given undesirable discharges because of civilian convictions for offenses committed off base. The general disqualification of persons convicted of serious felony crimes would bar some of these individuals from relief under this program, but those convicted for less serious civilian offenses would still be eligible.

**See pages 51–53.

Recommendation 33:
Individuals discharged for nonabsence offenses against
military discipline should be treated as follows:
(1) individuals with undesirable discharges should be
issued general discharges;
(2) a case-by-case review should determine whether
pardons and general discharges should be issued to
individuals discharged by general court-martial;
(3) a case-by-case review should determine whether pardons and general discharges should be issued to individuals discharged by special court-martial for offenses which (a) occurred in Vietnam, or (b) were
occasioned by orders to report for Vietnam;
(4) other individuals discharged by special court-martial
should be issued pardons and general discharges.

Former Servicemen with General Discharges (300,000)

General discharges defy easy description. They were given to
300,000 Vietnam-era servicemen whose records were considered
neither good enough to justify fully honorable discharges, nor
bad enough to warrant undesirable discharges or worse. Some
soldiers who received general discharges either had a long history of minor infractions or else committed major offenses but
were given light punishment because of strong extenuating circumstances. But general discharges were also given for reasons
wholly unrelated to discipline; they were used to "fire" servicemen who were incapable of performing satisfactorily because of
physical, mental, or psychological disabilities.

In practice, there was often no precise distinction between
soldiers who received general discharges and those who received
better or worse discharges. Given the variations in discharge
policies among military bases and commanding officers, general
discharges were given to many soldiers who might have deserved
better and to others who might well have received worse.

Many general discharges were given after unsuitability/unfitness
hearings which could have resulted in undesirable discharges. In
military shorthand, a general discharge for unsuitability was
given to those with aptitude problems—"who would if they
could, but they can't." An undesirable discharge for unfitness
went to soldiers with attitude problems—"who could if they

would, but they won't." To make this decision properly, a commanding officer had to know when poor performance was the
result of mental or psychological disabilities, a difficult judgment even for a skilled psychiatrist.

As the Vietnam War approached its end, administrative hearings became more and more lenient. Many of the same soldiers
who once would have gotten undesirable discharges received
general discharges instead. The Army increased its general discharge rate from 1.7 percent in 1969 to 8.2 percent in 1975,
while curtailing sharply its practice of giving undesirable discharges for unfitness.*

Former servicemen with general discharges are disadvantaged
by having a not-fully-honorable certificate, but they automatically qualify for veterans' benefits if they served the requisite
period of active duty. Surveys indicate that only 5 percent of
all employers refuse to hire them, whereas 35 to 50 percent
refuse to hire anyone with undesirable, bad-conduct, or dishonorable discharges. Thus, individuals with general discharges
do not present a pressing case for relief in a new program.

A case-by-case review of the 300,000 Vietnam-era general
discharges would entail enormous resources for a comparatively
marginal improvement in the status of these individuals. Nor
would it be advisable to grant them honorable discharges as a
class, for many of them did not perform well enough to deserve
such a commendation. Former servicemen with general discharges who believe they warrant honorable discharges can apply for upgrades through military discharge review boards, which
can give each case the individual attention it requires.

A special program focusing on Vietnam-era offenders should
not offer relief to veterans with general discharges. If they are
to be helped as a class, it should be through a fundamental
restructuring of the military discharge system.

> *Recommendation 34:*
> Individuals now holding general discharges should not
> be extended relief under this program.

---

*The total proportion of undesirable discharges has not reflected this
change because of the increasingly common use of undesirable discharges
"for the good of the service" in lieu of court-martial. These latter discharges are not given through unsuitability/unfitness hearings.

Applicants to President Ford's Clemency Program (21,800)

The Ford program complicates the formulation of a new approach because it raises questions of equity for persons who participated in that earlier program. These 21,800 individuals can be divided into four main groups: (1) the 6,000 who received the full measure of relief under the Ford program without having to perform alternative service; (2) the 2,500 who will receive relief after completing alternative service; (3) the 11,000 who were offered conditional clemency but will not complete their assigned service; and (4) the 1,000 who were denied relief.*

(1) Convicted draft offenders who were offered immediate relief without alternative service received pardons; former servicemen received pardons and clemency discharges. The Ford pardons were never defined and are thus of uncertain effect. The president should define his pardons carefully in a new program, making it clear that he wishes pardons under the prior program to be regarded in the new manner. Those who received clemency discharges without having to perform alternative service should automatically be granted general discharges through the new program, since their cases have already been favorably acted upon by the Clemency Board and President Ford. However, eligibility for veterans' benefits should be decided according to the standards of the new program.

(2) Those who earned clemency under the Ford program by performing alternative service should receive at least the same relief as everyone else under the new program. The question is whether they should be given credit for completing that service. Nothing extra can be offered civilians, since the dismissal of pending prosecutions, the granting of pardons, and the sealing of the official records leaves little room for additional relief. However, former servicemen who completed alternative service under the Ford program should have the length of this service taken into account in calculating whether their period of military service warrants eligibility for veterans' benefits. The presidential task force should establish guide-

*These four groups do not include about 700 Clemency Board recommendations still pending before the president, and 500 Clemency Board applicants who submitted insufficient information to enable their case files to be located.

lines for the weight to be given alternative service in making these calculations.

(3) All people who were offered conditional clemency but later dropped out of the program should be included in a new program. The Ford program considered them worthy of relief after careful review of the facts in their cases, and these prior determinations should be given full effect. The fact that they were unable or unwilling to perform alternative service should be disregarded in a program which itself imposes no conditions of this kind.

(4) The only persons denied relief under the Ford program were fugitive military offenders who had committed serious nonabsence offenses* and applicants to the Clemency Board whose cases involved especially serious aggravating factors, such as violent felony crimes or combat-related desertion offenses. These cases should be treated in accordance with the standards of the new program. Persons qualifying for automatic relief under these standards sould receive it, nowithstanding the judgments of the Ford program. Those whose cases fall into categories requiring case-by-case review should be evaluated anew, with no weight given to the earlier decision.

> *Recommendation 35:*
> Applicants to the Ford clemency program who were granted immediate clemency or offered conditional clemency should automatically be given relief under the new program. Those denied relief by the Ford program should be given relief according to the standards of the new program.

Implementation

The Initiative for a Program

Theoretically, a program of relief could come as a result of presidential or legislative action. Although the Constitution vests the pardoning power in the president, the text itself does

---

*These individuals were directed to report to a nearby base for disposition of these other charges. Although they were not placed in custody, most did as directed and were eventually able to avoid court-martial by accepting undesirable discharges.

not suggest that the amnesty power is exclusively executive in nature. Largely as a result of congressional interest in a post-Vietnam amnesty, a number of authorities have argued that Congress may pass amnesty legislation of its own. No Supreme Court case has ruled unequivocally on the question of congressional authority, but the Court has upheld previous legislation which granted immunity or relief to certain classes of persons. In the *Brown* v. *Walker* case, the Court declared that "although the Court vests in the President 'power to grant reprieves and pardons for offenses against the United States, except in cases of impeachment,' this power has never been held to take from Congress the power to pass acts of general amnesty." Despite this language, scholars differ in their interpretation of the *Brown* case, and some are skeptical about whether Congress possesses an independent amnesty power comparable to the pardon power of the president.

As a practical matter, it appears unlikely that there is sufficient congressional support to produce amnesty legislation in the face of opposition or disinterest on the part of the president. In the immediate future, a program of relief will come, if at all, as a result of a presidential initiative. Almost all aspects of a desirable program can be accomplished within the framework of the Constitutional authority granted the president under Article II, Section 2, supplemented by his authority as commander-in-chief.

Congressional participation in the program would involve obvious risks. Unilateral executive decision-making would have to give way to a much more complicated political process whose outcome might be uncertain. But Congressional participation would provide an opportunity to air the amnesty issue in its full context, to clarify popular misconceptions, and mobilize public support behind the program.

Specifically, legislative action also would be necessary in four areas:

(1) The president is limited by law in the funding and administration of any special program not authorized by Congress. Resources either have to come from the president's unanticipated needs budget or from the budgets of other executive agencies. The Ford clemency program was supported in these ways, resulting in a number of management problems. The Clemency Board had to recruit its entire 600-person staff through short-

term details from other agencies. Since the president's discretionary budget could not be used for more than one year, the Clemency Board had to go out of business before all its work was done, and a follow-up program was hastily organized under new leadership in the Justice Department. To assure that the administration of a new program would have independent staff resources for as long as necessary to complete its tasks, and to avoid legal complications if the program is to be funded for more than one year, the president would have to seek authorization and appropriations from Congress.

(2) Legislative action offers the best means of restoring the citizenship rights of Vietnam-era offenders who have lost their American citizenship. Although this problem might be addressed administratively by reinterpreting the standards which determine the voluntariness of the individual's act of expatriation, a more straightforward approach requires legislative action.

(3) While the president may direct that executive branch records be sealed and kept confidential, he has no power over records possessed by the federal judiciary, state and local governments, and the private sector. Legislative authority would be necessary to seal those records.

> *Recommendation 36:*
> The program should be a presidential initiative.

> *Recommendation 37:*
> A legislative proposal should be submitted to Congress requesting (1) authorization and appropriations for the program; (2) provisions for the sealing of records held by the federal judiciary, state and local governments, and the private sector; and (3) special exceptions to the immigration law enabling expatriates to restore their American citizenship.

Responsibility for the Program's Administration

To give a new program proper visibility, independence, and disassociation from past policies, a presidential task force should be appointed to make plans, determine policies, and oversee the implementation of the entire program. This task force should report directly to the president and its authority should be derived from his personal mandate.

The task force should consist of five individuals with distinguished backgrounds in public service. The chairman should have sufficient stature to act as a public spokesman for the entire program and as the personal representative of the president.

All five members of the task force should work full-time on the program during its planning phase. Thereafter, the chairman should remain in personal control of the entire program, assisted by other members of the task force whenever necessary. The task force should be aided by a small staff which could be increased as needs dictate, and it should have independent hiring authority to fill professional positions. The task force should be financed through the president's unanticipated needs fund until Congress authorizes the program and appropriates necessary funds.

The work of the task force, and the administration of the entire program, would come in three phases. The *planning phase* should last no more than three months. During this period, the task force should establish the policies and administrative details of the program. It should define the rights and benefits afforded categories of individuals. All members of the task force should spend several weeks reviewing and deciding actual cases to become familiar with basic fact patterns. They should develop suitable procedural safeguards, designate criteria for making case-by-case decision, and establish precedents for applying those criteria. The task force should also develop the necessary lines of authority for controlling the functions performed by the Justice Department, Defense Department, and Veterans Administration. Steps must be taken to ensure that all government agencies conform their practices and policies with the standards set by the program. Policy decisions and guidelines developed by the task force should be subject to public review and comment in accordance with the principles of the Administrative Procedures Act.

The *implementation phase* should be completed within a year. The chairman of the task force must remain in direct control of this phase of the program. Three major efforts would have to be undertaken. First, the Justice Department and Defense Department must conduct a complete review of existing official records, making the necessary changes in status, identifying cases which require separate treatment, and notifying individuals of the actions taken in their cases. This would be a time-consuming process, requiring a substantial commitment of clerical resources. Second, the Justice Department, Defense Department, and Veterans Administration should make case-by-case decisions through suitable adjudicative mechanisms. The chairman, assisted by other members of the task force, should review these decisions, and have the power to reverse them, to ensure that they are consistent with the guidelines and spirit of the program. The task force must have the power to reverse case-by-case decisions. Third, a public information campaign must be implemented to advise beneficiaries of the rights and benefits provided by the program. This campaign should include public statements by the president and members of the task force, direct communications with program beneficiaries, and dissemination of information about the program to the general public.

A *follow-up phase* would be necessary following completion of the major work of the program. The task force should issue a comprehensive public report, summarizing its activities, stating its major findings about Vietnam-era offenders, and making such recommendations with respect to future policies as it deems advisable. Because there would be no deadlines for individuals who must make individual application for relief, some provision must be made for processing their cases and performing other residual tasks.

The Justice Department, Defense Department, and Veterans Administration have information, expertise, and administrative responsibilities essential to the implementation of the program. An advisory committee, with one representative from each agency, should be created to assist the task force in implementing the program.

Recommendation 38:
A task force reporting directly to the president should be established to plan and oversee the implementation of the program.

Recommendation 39:
An advisory committee, consisting of representatives from the Defense Department, Justice Department, and Veterans Administration should be established to assist the presidential task force.

Recommendation 40:
The presidential task force should issue a public report at the close of its operations, offering such recommendations with respect to draft and military discipline as it deems advisable.

Personal Involvement of the President

The effective implementation of this program requires that the president take an active personal role. He should maintain a close relationship with the task force, taking whatever steps are necessary to assure that the program is effectively implemented.

The president also has a visible public role to play to help the program ease the bitter feelings of the Vietnam era. Through speeches and public statements, he could correct the public's misconceptions about draft and military offenders and help to encourage their reintegration into society. Until the American people accept them as equal members of society, Vietnam-era offenders will continue to have trouble finding jobs, qualifying for credit, or enjoying other social and economic privileges. For this program to achieve a true reconciliation, the president would have to exercise the strongest possible moral leadership.

Recommendation 41:
The president should take an active public role in the program.

5. Beyond the Program

The situation of draft and military offenders illustrates the severity of the personal impact of Vietnam-era military manpower policies. The evidence strongly suggests that the draft was inequitable, federal prosecutions ineffective, and military discharge policies overly harsh. Strong efforts should be made to avoid similar problems if America's youth are again called upon to fight a war. The implementation of a program for Vietnam-era offenders should stimulate a careful reassessment of these policies.

Conscription Policies

If the draft is judged only according to its ability to provide the required manpower to fight the Vietnam War, it can be considered successful. But as a fair mechanism for allocating the the burdens of war, it proved a failure. Millions of individuals deliberately avoided military duty, hundreds of thousands failed to register for the draft, tens of thousands escaped prosecution through technical defenses, and only a few thousand were punished. While much of the resistance to conscription can be traced to the public opposition to the war, it would be a mistake to ascribe the problems of the draft totally to Vietnam. The draft was administered by a network of local boards, state headquarters, and national officials who were unable to satisfy the court-imposed requirements of due process. The consequence was a progressive breakdown in the enforcement of the draft laws.

This could easily happen again. The draft lottery solved only part of the problem. America cannot safely assume that a future emergency requiring a return to conscription would not produce the same turmoil as the Vietnam era—widespread avoidance, the emergence of a network of draft counseling, due process violations by draft boards, sporadic criminal enforcement, and general public discontent.

With the termination of the draft and the recent reliance on a volunteer army, little contingency planning has gone into how a new system of conscription would operate. As has too often been the case in our history, the nation may resume where it left off, relying on Selective Service policies as they existed at the end of the war and adjusting those inherited policies hastily in the midst of a new crisis. As difficult and distasteful as it may be to consider the outlines of new military manpower policies while memories of the past are so sharp, defense preparedness demands that the following questions be answered:

Who should bear the brunt of battle in time of limited mobilization—conscripted, volunteer, or reserve forces?

How can military service be allocated equitably throughout the affected generation, especially when full mobilization is not required?

Can an alternative be found to replace the present Selective Service System concept of local boards for administering a system of conscription?

Can a draft system's administrative discretion be reduced or even eliminated while still taking due account of the principle of conscientious objection?

Can the criminal justice system's enforcement of the draft laws be improved?

Military Discharge Policies

Increasing recognition of the impact of bad discharges has prompted a number of changes in military policy since the end of the Vietnam War. The postdischarge review mechanism has been expanded, primarily through regionalization of the discharge review boards, to provide wider access to individuals who wish to have their discharges upgraded. This has been accompanied by a proliferation of private counseling organizations to assist former servicemen in having their discharges improved. The result has been a clear liberalizing trend.

New policies have been adopted to identify and discharge promptly soldiers who demonstrate an inability to provide satisfactory service before they commit offenses serious enough to require courts-martial and disciplinary discharges. Through these new policies, general or honorable certificates are issued to the same kinds of soldiers who formerly would have received undesirable discharges or worse. These post-Vietnam "early-out" policies are experimental and, according to the prevailing military view, valid only for a pacetime, volunteer armed force.

These changes reflect an expanding awareness of the long-term social and economic costs of characterizing military service by grade-discharge certificates. A comprehensive program of relief for Vietnam-era offenders would accelerate this trend by acknowledging that, for the most recent generation of soldiers, these costs have been too high. Several questions should be asked about possible changes in the present discharge system:

Can military discipline be effectively served without relying on the deterrent or incentive quality of discharges?

Are there special awards and certificates, other than discharges, which can convey the military's judgment that a soldier's performance has been of truly "honorable" or exceptionally good quality?

Can the discharge system be changed to eliminate the permanent social and economic disabilities suffered by those who perform unsatisfactorily?

Can the present discharge system be replaced by one which does not publicly characterize performance but merely indicates the length of military service and, in the case of those discharged by court-martial, the fact that separation was by reason of criminal conviction?

Can the permanent detrimental effects of discharge certificates be removed by a system of automatic recharacterization after a period of time?

The Broader Lessons of Vietnam

This program of relief for Vietnam-era offenders would focus only on the burdens faced by one category of Americans. By restoring their rights and removing their stigmas, it would resolve one of the last controversial issues from the war. Yet it would not address the needs of all Vietnam-era veterans. Nothing can be done for those who died, and those who were severely injured can never be made whole again. But the efforts they put forward deserve more recognition and more understanding than America has shown thus far. All Vietnam veterans have borne much of the price of the popular desire to forget Vietnam as quickly as possible. Perhaps this program would awaken the nation to this broader problem, providing impetus for more compassionate policies for all veterans of the Vietnam War.

APPENDIX

TABLE 1

HISTORY OF MAJOR PRESIDENTIAL AMNESTIES

President	Date	Benefits
Washington	July 10, 1795	"Full, free and entire" pardons to all insurrectionists involved in Whiskey Rebellion except those under indictment
John Adams	May 21, 1800	Pardons to all insurrectionists involved in the Fries Rebellion except those under indictment or standing convicted
Jefferson	October 15, 1807	Full Pardons to all deserters who surrendered to the military and returned to duty
Madison	1812–1814	Three proclamations pardoning deserters who returned to military duty
	February 6, 1815	Pardons for those pirates of Jean Lafitte who aided General Jackson against the British at the battle of New Orleans
Jackson	June 12, 1830	Deserters under sentence of death and fugitives were discharged from the army and barred from future enlistment; those under arrest for desertion were returned to duty
Lincoln	December 8, 1863	Pardons to Confederate soldiers willing to subscribe to an oath of allegiance to the U.S.
	February 26, 1864	Sentences of all deserters condemned to death mitigated to imprisonment for duration of Civil War (141 Union deserters had already been executed)
	March 11, 1865	Pardons to deserters who returned to duty within sixty days and served for a period of time equal to their original enlistments (Deserters who did not respond to

TABLE 1 (contd)

President	Date	Benefits
		Lincoln's offer were deemed to have "voluntarily relinquished and forfeited their rights to citizenship")
Johnson	1865–1868; a series of Proclamations	Extended rights provided to Confederate rebels in the December 8, 1863, Lincoln pardon
Harding	Christmas, 1921	Commuted term of socialist Eugene V. Debs after Debs had served three years of a ten-year sentence for violating the Sedition Act of 1918
Coolidge	December 15, 1923	Pardoned thirty-one federal prisoners who had been convicted under the Espionage Act of opposing the government and Selective Service during World War I
F. D. Roosevelt	December 23, 1933	Restored civil rights to about 1,500 persons who had completed prison terms for violating the Draft and Espionage Acts during World War I
Truman	Christmas, 1945	Restored citizenship rights to several thousand ex-convicts who had served at least one year in the military after July 28, 1941, and were subsequently awarded Honorable Discharges
	December 23, 1946	Amnesty Board case-by-case review of 15,805 persons sentenced for violating the Selective Service Act; 1,523 were granted pardons, all but three of whom had completed their prison terms
	Christmas, 1952	Restored civil rights to 8,940 persons convicted of deserting during peacetime—between August 15, 1945 and June 25, 1950 (no par-

TABLE 1 (contd)

President	Date	Benefits
		don, remission or mitigation of sentence involved)
	Christmas, 1952	Restored civil rights to Korean War veterans who had been convicted in civil courts prior to their military service
Ford	September 16, 1974	(See Chapter 3 of this report)

Source: The Presidential Clemency Board Report, p. 345.

TABLE 2

CHARACTERISTICS OF VIETNAM-ERA
DRAFT AND MILITARY ABSENCE OFFENDERS
(all figures in percentages)

	Draft Convicted	Military Discharged	Military Fugitives
A. BACKGROUND			
Race			
White	87	75	80
Black	10	20	20
Other	3	5	
Family Background			
Both parents	69	52	
One parent	26	41	
No parents	5	7	
Childhood Residence			
Urban	58	47	
Suburban	19	12	
Rural small town	18	32	
Rural farm	6	9	
Childhood Region			
East	21	23	23
South	19	32	33
Midwest	28	31	32
West	32	14	19
Education			
Non-high school graduate	20	71	64
High school graduate	33	20	29
Beyond high school	47	9	7
IQ			
1–90	19	39	
91–109	27	39	
110+	54	23	

TABLE 2 (contd)

	Draft Convicted	Military Discharged	Military Fugitives
Armed Forces Qualifying Test			
I (93–100 percentile)		7	2
II (65–92 percentile)		19	16
III (31–64 percentile)		45	43
IV & V (0–30 percentile)		29	39
Religion			
Jehovah's Witness	21	0	
Other pacifist religion	7	0.4	
Nonpacifist religion or no religion	72	99	

B. DRAFT HISTORY

CO Application

No evidence noted	56
Some initiative	11
CO denied	24
CO granted	10

Type of Draft Offense

Failure to register	3
Failure to keep draft board notified	10
Failure to submit to induction	34
Failure to show for physical	4
Failure to show for induction	35
Failure to complete alternate service	15

Primary Motivation for Draft Offense

Antiwar	80
Personal/family problems	10
Unfairness	8
Incapacity	2

TABLE 2 (contd)

	Draft Convicted	Military Discharged	Military Fugitives
Year of Offense			
1964–65	1		
1966–67	3		
1968–69	19		
1970–71	53		
1972–73	24		
Region of Conviction			
East	17		
South	19		
Midwest	27		
West	37		
Months Incarcerated for Draft Offense			
0	67		
1–6	15		
7–12	5		
13–24	10		
25–72	3		

C. MILITARY HISTORY

	Draft Convicted	Military Discharged	Military Fugitives
Age of Entry			
16–17		31	14
18–19		47	45
20–21		16	24
22 +		6	18
Military Intake			
Draft		19	43
Enlistee		81	55
Reserves		—	2
Reason for Enlistment			
"Get away from problems"		32*	
"To see what the army is like"		27*	

*Army AWOL study (see end of tables).

TABLE 2 (contd)

	Draft Convicted	Military Discharged	Military Fugitives
"The draft would get me"		26*	
"To learn a skill"		21*	
"Had nothing else to do"		17*	
"Forced by a judge"		15*	
"Always wanted to be a soldier"		9*	
Branch of Service			
Army		62	
Marines		23	
Navy		12	
Air Force		3	
Other		0.1	
Vietnam Service			
Yes		27	19
No		73	81
Type of Vietnam Service			
None		73	
Tour ended in AWOL		2	
Tour ended in injury		2	
Other reason for tour end		3	
Full tour		16	
More than one tour		3	
Location of Vietnam Service			
Combat		81	
Saigon		1	
Elsewhere noncombat		18	
Highest Rank			
E-1		20*	40
E-2		26*	27
E-3		18*	15
E-4		22*	12
E-5		12*	5
E-6		2*	
Months of Military Service			
less than 1		1	

*Army AWOL study (see end of tables)

TABLE 2 (contd)

	Draft Convicted	Military Discharged	Military Fugitives
1–6		19	
7–12		22	
13–24		29	
25–36		17	
over 36		12	
Type of Absence Offense			
AWOL		90	
Desertion*		9	
Other		1	
Location of Base			
Continental U.S.			88
Europe			5
Vietnam			5
Other overseas			3
Primary Motivation for Offense			
Personal/family/financial		64	50
Adjustment problems		16	27
Objection to war		7	12
Service mismanagement		12	9
Other		2	3
Circumstances of Last Absence Offense			
Left training		17	
Left U.S. duty unrelated to Vietnam		46	
Left U.S. duty upon orders to Vietnam		7	
No return to Vietnam after leave		2	
Left noncombat area in Vietnam		2	
Left combat in Vietnam		1	
Left U.S. duty after Vietnam		25	
Duty Station Upon Leaving			
Training			24
Garrison			31
Leave/convalescence			20
Transit			18
Confinement			6
Combat			1

*Servicemen found guilty of desertion offenses

TABLE 2 (contd)

	Draft Convicted	Military Discharged	Military Fugitives
Number of Previous Absence Offenses			
0		12	
1		25	
2		23	
3		18	
4		11	
5+		11	
Months Incarcerated			
0		51	
1–6		40	
7–12		8	
12+		1	
Type of Discharge			
Undesirable in lieu of court-martial		43	
Undesirable—unfitness		16	
Bad conduct		38	
Dishonorable		2	
Age at Discharge			
16–17		1	
18–19		14	
20–21		38	
22–23		27	
24+		21	

D. EXPERIENCE AS FUGITIVES

	Draft Convicted	Military Discharged	Military Fugitives
Activity While Fugitive			
No attempt to hide	85	88	87
Attempt to hide	15	12	13
Place While Fugitive			
U.S.	88	90	89
Canada	7	2	7
Other foreign country	5	8	3

TABLE 2 (contd)

	Draft Convicted	Military Discharged	Military Fugitives
Employment While Fugitive			
Full time	69	82	85
Part time	24	10	11
Unemployed	7	8	3
Problems Caused by Fugitive Status			
None			64
Some:			36
employment			(13)
family/marital			(12)
drugs			(6)
other			(5)

E. PRESENT STATUS

Family Status

	Draft Convicted	Military Discharged	Military Fugitives
Single	49	41	38
Was married	7	6 ⎤	
Married, no dependents	24	15 ⎥	62
Married, dependents	21	38 ⎦	

Mental/Physical Problems

None	87	72	
Physical, no disability	3	4	
Physical, disabled	2	3	
Psychological problem	7	15	
Drug problem	2	5	
Alcohol problem	1	1	

Other Civilian Convictions

None	96	88	
Nonviolent felony	3	6	
Violent felony	1	6	

TABLE 2 (contd)

	Draft Convicted	Military Discharged	Military Fugitives
Present Employment Status			
Employed full-time	88	69	
Employed part-time	9	14	
Unemployed	3	17	

Sources: All "Military Fugitive" statistics come from *The Vietnam Era Deserter: Charac-teristics of Unconvicted Army Deserters Participating in the Presidential Clemency Pro-gram,* a study conducted by D. Bruce Bell and Thomas J. Houston for the Army Research Institute for the Behavioral and Social Sciences. Except when indicated by an asterisk, "Military Convicted" statistics come from the Clemency Board's survey of 1,009 partici-pants in its program. Asterisked statistics are extracted from *Leadership and Situational Factors Related to AWOL: A Research Repo1t* by Hamilton I. McCubbin, July, 1971. "Draft Convicted" statistics come from the Clemency Board's survey of 472 draft of-fenders who participated in its program.

TABLE 3

TYPES OF DISCHARGES ISSUED TO ENLISTED PERSONNEL DURING VIETNAM ERA (FY 1965-1974)

Year	Honorable	Percent	General	Percent	Un-desirable	Percent	Bad Conduct	Per-cent	Dishon-orable	Per-cent	Total Discharged
1965	678,100	94.3	25,477	3.5	13,178	1.8	2,088	.3	55	.0	718,898
1966	705,761	95.5	10,883	2.8	10,544	1.4	1,784	.2	72	.0	740,044
1967	657,684	95.4	19,562	2.8	9,741	1.4	2,565	.4	65	.0	689,617
1968	836,990	96.2	18,260	2.1	11,707	1.3	2,886	.3	34	.0	869,877
1969	980,376	96.4	19,853	2.0	12,392	1.2	3,662	.4	187	.0	1,016,470
1970	1,081,556	95.2	29,334	2.6	20,911	1.8	3,964	.3	375	.0	1,136,140
1971	944,365	92.7	40,256	4.0	29,139	2.9	4,737	.5	325	.0	1,018,822
1972	804,470	90.3	45,219	5.1	36,345	4.1	4,167	.5	356	.0	890,557
1973	646,720	89.8	40,680	5.7	29,049	4.0	2,906	.4	434	.1	719,789
1974	609,580	83.6	45,960	6.7	29,336	4.3	2,988	.4	315	.0	688,179

Vietnam-Era Less-than-Honorable Discharges

General	305,475
Undesirable	202,342)
Bad Conduct	31,747)
Dishonorable	2,218)
TOTAL:	541,782

236,307 discharges under other-than-honorable conditions

Source: Selected Manpower Statistics, Department of Defense, May 1975.

TABLE 4

TOTAL DISCHARGES FOR THE GOOD OF THE SERVICE
IN LIEU OF COURT-MARTIAL***
FY 1967–1975

	Army	Navy	Marine Corps	Air Force	Total
1967	294	**	1*	129	424
1968	384	**	7*	370	761
1969	532	**	471*	425	1,428
1970	6,993	**	3,351	386	10,730
1971	12,041	214	4,704	557	17,516
1972	25,515	1,363	1,825	915	29,618
1973	21,066	1,657	1,684	475	24,882
1974	17,672	2,266	2,728	285	22,951
1975	14,784	2,790	3,437	601	21,612

*Calendar year
**Not used in Navy prior April 1971
***Approximately 90 percent of these are undesirable discharges

Source: Department of Defense, Office of Manpower and Reserve Affairs.

TABLE 5

VIETNAM-ERA COURT-MARTIAL RATES IN THE ARMED FORCES*

FY	65	66	67	68	69	70	71	72	73
General Courts-Martial** Total:	2,298	2,089	2,746	3,498	3,712	4,178	3,684	2,929	2,418
Rate/1000 servicemen	.9	.7	.8	1.0	1.1	1.4	1.3	1.2	1.0
Special Courts-Martial** Total:	40,274	39,593	54,129	61,525	77,569	58,615	41,032	26,451	24,643
Rate/1000 servicemen	15.1	12.8	16.0	17.3	22.4	19.1	14.2	10.5	10.6
Total General and Special Courts-Martial* Total:	42,572	41,682	56,587	65,023	81,281	62,793	44,716	29,380	27,061
Rate/1000 servicemen	16.0	13.5	16.8	18.3	23.5	20.5	15.5	11.7	11.6

*Does not include summary courts-martial
**Not all courts-martial resulted in discharges.

Source: Department of Defense Statistics, Judiciary Offices

TABLE 6

PERCENT OF DISCHARGES UNDER OTHER-THAN-HONORABLE
CONDITIONS ISSUED THROUGH ADMINISTRATIVE PROCEDURES*
(in percentages)

Fiscal Years	Army	Navy	Marines	Air Force	Total
1950–54	64.5	40.2	42.6	----	61.9
1955–59	78.9	59.7	45.2	78.8	77.4
1960–64	87.0	67.5	61.5	69.8	81.6
1965–69	87.2	69.8	54.3	73.6	81.1
1970–73	92.3	66.4	80.5	83.7	87.0

*Percentage of undesirable discharges of all undesirable, bad-conduct, and dis-honorable discharges.

Source: Extrapolations from Defense Department Discharge Statistics.

TABLE 7

VIETNAM-ERA ABSENTEE INCIDENT RATES COMPARED TO
WORLD WAR II AND KOREA
(Absentee Incidents of less than 30 days)

	Year	Army	Navy	Marine Corps	Air Force
World War II	CY 1942	*	*	*	(Air Force did
	CY 1943	*	*	*	not become a
	CY 1944	*	*	*	separate Service
	CY 1945	*	*	*	until 1947.)
Korea	FY 1951	*	28.4	*	*
	FY 1952	181.0	31.9	*	62.0
	FY 1953	158.0	36.3	*	58.44
	FY 1954	115.3	37.6	*	38.32
Vietnam	FY 1965	60.1	26.8	*	2.9
	FY 1966	57.2	29.2	*	3.3
	FY 1967	78.0	22.4	*	3.6
	FY 1968	89.7	14.4	*	3.6
	FY 1969	112.3	13.54	*	4.4
	FY 1970	132.5	17.5	174.3	5.9
	FY 1971	176.9	19.0	166.6	9.4
	FY 1972	166.4	18.3	170.0	17.2
	FY 1973	159.0	21.7	234.3	16.1
	FY 1974	130.0	53.8	287.5	17.3

Discussion:

Absentee Incident Rate: Rate per 1,000 average enlisted monthly end strength
* Data not available
CY Calendar year (January 1–December 31)
FY Fiscal year (July 1–June 30)

Source: Statistics from Department of Defense (Office of Manpower and Reserve Affairs).

TABLE 8

VIETNAM-ERA DESERTION RATES COMPARED TO
WORLD WAR II AND KOREA
(Unauthorized absence of 30 days or more)

	Year	Army	Navy	Marine Corps	Air Force
				1 Dec 41–	
World	CY 1942	*	5.5	30 Jun 42 7.3	(Air Force did
War II	CY 1943	*	3.1	FY 8.8	not become a
	CY 1944	63.0	3.0	FY 6.9	separate Service
	CY 1945	45.2	3.5	FY 5.4	until 1947.)
	FY 1951	CY 14.3	3.1	10.1	*
Korea	FY 1952	22.0	6.2	19.7	*
	FY 1953	22.3	8.7	29.6	*
	FY 1954	15.7	6.9	July 53 - 2.2	*
	FY 1965	15.7	6.7	18.8	.39
	FY 1966	14.7	9.1	16.1	.35
	FY 1967	21.4	9.7	26.8	.42
	FY 1968	29.1	8.5	30.7	.44
Vietnam	FY 1969	42.4	7.34	40.2	.63
	FY 1970	52.3	9.9	59.6	.80
	FY 1971	73.5	11.1	56.2	1.5
	FY 1972	62.0	8.8	65.3	2.8
	FY 1973	52.0	13.6	63.2	2.2
	FY 1974	41.2	21.2	89.2	2.4

Discussion:

Desertion: The term used herein has no legal significance. When an individual has been absent without authority for thirty days or more, he is administratively classified as a deserter. Only after an individual is convicted of the charge of desertion can the term "deserter" be applied in the full legal sense.

Desertion Rate: Rate per 1,000 average enlisted monthly end strength.

* Data not available

CY Calendar year (January 1–December 31)

FY Fiscal year (July 1–June 30)

Source: Statistics from Department of Defense (Office of Manpower and Reserve Affairs).

TABLE 9

VIETNAM-ERA ARMY COURTS-MARTIAL FOR AWOL
AND DESERTION COMPARED TO WORLD WAR II AND KOREA

AWOL

Period	Tried	Convicted	Rate*	Average Strength
FY 1942–47	29,239	28,436	6.0	4,848,000
1951–53**	2,320	2,229	1.6	1,408,000
FY 1964–71	9,582	9,398	7.4	1,294,000

DESERTION

Period	Tried	Convicted	Rate*	Average Strength
FY 1942–47	21,049	20,392	4.3	4,848,000
1951–53**	8,485	3,369	6.0	1,408,000
FY 1964–71	1,491	960	1.2	1,294,000

*The rate of tried cases per thousand average strength.
**Covers the period May 1, 1951, through May 31, 1953.

Source: Clerk of Court, United States Army Judiciary, Falls Church, Virginia.

128

TABLE 10

IMPACT OF LESS-THAN-HONORABLE DISCHARGES
ON EMPLOYMENT OPPORTUNITIES
(in percentages)

Bradley Jones's 1973 Survey of Businesses,
Colleges and Professional Associations

	Less Likely to Hire	Automatic Reject
General discharge	51	8
Undesirable discharge	69	20
Bad-conduct discharge	75	27
Dishonorable discharge	77	34

William Pearman's 1975 Study on the Impact of
the Ford Clemency Program on Employment Prospects

	Less Likely to Hire	Automatic Reject
Honorable discharge	0	0
General discharge	39	5
Undesirable discharge	75	34
Dishonorable discharge	79	52
Clemency discharge	47	18
Clemency discharge with alternative service	40	12
Civilian draft offender with presidential pardon—no alternative service	57	16
Civilian draft offender with presidential pardon—with alternative service	41	12

Sources: Jones Study—*Military Law Review* 53 (Winter, 1973), p. 1.
Pearman Study—*Clemency Board Report*, p. 403.

TABLE 11

OVERVIEW OF SELECTIVE SERVICE VIOLATIONS

	Draft Calls	SSS Complaints	Defendants	Convictions	Imprisonment	Average Sentence of those Imprisoned (months)
1963	70,000	11,793	—	—	—	—
1964	145,000	13,589	—	—	—	—
1965	102,600	13,661	341	242	189	21.0
1966	334,530	13,835	517	372	302	—
1967	288,900	19,774	996	748	666	32.1
1968	343,300	21,331	1,192	784	580	37.3
1969	266,900	27,444	1,744	900	544	36.3
1970	209,300	26,475	2,833	1,027	450	33.5
1971	152,000	25,504	2,973	1,036	377	29.1
1972	41,000	20,091	4,906	1,642	458	22.0
1973	35,000	13,278	3,495	977	260	17.5
1974	—	2,742	2,094	799	155	14.5
1975	—	—	1,376	229	20	
Total:	1,988,530	209,517	22,467	8,756	4,001	—

Source: Federal Offenders in United States District Courts, Administrative Office of the U.S. Courts.

TABLE 12

STATUS OF SELECTIVE SERVICE COMPLAINTS, 1967-70* (SELECTED DISTRICTS)

Prosecutorial District	Number of cases	Number Indicted	Number Dropped	Percent Indicted**	Percent Dropped**
Virgin Islands	89	3	85	3	96
South Carolina	708	64	682	9	96
New York (southern)	6,006	155	5,688	3	95
California (southern)	3,395	118	3,183	3	94
Mississippi (northern)	388	23	364	6	94
New York (eastern)	10,886	256	10,109	2	93
North Carolina (eastern)	893	53	817	6	91
North Carolina (central)	465	38	420	8	90
Illinois (northern)	1,173	380	543	32	46
Oregon	1,031	365	470	35	46
Ohio (northern)	630	254	273	40	43
Idaho	104	47	41	45	39
Maine	90	51	19	56	21
Missouri (western)	228	148	38	65	17
Puerto Rico	204	97	25	48	12
Tennessee (central)	39	36	2	92	5
New Hampshire	75	71	2	95	3
National Total:	94,774	10,383	75,939	11	80

*Data is only available for these years.

**This does not add up to 100 percent, ordinarily because of cases which remained pending at the time this data was published. The South Carolina percentages exceed 100 percent because of a case backlog which existed in 1967.

Source: Department of Justice, Hearings before the House Armed Services Committee, Subcommittee on the Draft, 91st Congress, 2d Session (1970), pp. 12858-60.

TABLE 13

YEAR-BY-YEAR CONVICTION AND IMPRISONMENT
PERCENTAGES FOR SELECTIVE SERVICE VIOLATORS
(in percentages)

Fiscal Year	Convicted of all defendants	Imprisoned of all convicted	Imprisoned of all defendants
1965	71.0	78.0	55.4
1966	72.0	81.2	58.4
1967	75.1	89.0	66.6
1968	65.8	73.9	48.6
1969	51.6	60.4	31.1
1970	36.3	43.8	15.8
1971	34.8	36.3	12.7
1972	33.5	27.8	9.3
1973	28.0	26.6	7.4
1974	38.2	19.3	7.4
1975	16.6	8.7	1.4

Source: Extrapolations from *Federal Offenders in United States District Courts,* Administrative Office of the U.S. Courts.

TABLE 14

DRAFT PROSECUTIONS: VARIATIONS OVER TIME
(SELECTED DISTRICT COURTS)

	*Defendants**	*Convicted*	*Imprisoned*
Massachusetts			
1966–69	74	39 (53%)	30 (41%)
1970–74	231	68 (29%)	26 (11%)
Connecticut			
1966–69	36	23 (64%)	19 (53%)
1970–74	147	19 (13%)	3 (2%)
Michigan (eastern)			
1966–69	85	59 (70%)	57 (67%)
1970–74	877	225 (26%)	31 (4%)
Wisconsin (eastern)			
1966–69	86	43 (50%)	39 (45%)
1970–74	243	45 (19%)	13 (5%)
New Jersey			
1966–69	160	79 (40%)	44 (28%)
1970–74	400	156 (39%)	4 (1%)
California (north)			
1966–69	232	173 (75%)	88 (38%)
1970–74	1759	587 (33%)	124 (7%)

*Indicted persons only.

Source: Extrapolations from *Federal Offenders in United States District Courts,* Administrative Office of the U.S. Courts.

TABLE 15

FEDERAL DISTRICT CONVICTION AND IMPRISONMENT RATES
FOR INDICTED DRAFT OFFENDERS OVER TEN-YEAR PERIOD, 1966-1975
(VARIATIONS IN SELECTED DISTRICTS)

	Number of defendants	Percent convicted	Percent imprisoned	Percent imprisoned over three years
Mississippi (southern)	38	66	58	48
Texas (western)	199	62	47	37
Florida (middle)	318	58	37	8
Indiana (southern)	231	47	21	7
New Jersey	600	39	8	5
North Carolina (eastern)	196	37	27	22
New York (southern)	589	37	16	3
California (northern)	2,099	36	10	0.8
Alabama (northern)	74	36	5	1
Michigan (eastern)	1,061	30	8	6
Connecticut	203	22	11	6
Puerto Rico	120	6	4	0

Source: Extrapolations from *Federal Offenders in United States District Courts*, Administrative Office of the U.S. Courts.

TABLE 16

DRAFT CONVICTIONS COMPARED TO OTHER CRIMES
(in percentages)

	Draft Offenses	Violent Crimes*	Property Crimes*
Offenders Identified**	100	100	100
Offenders Charged	12	80	86
Offenders Convicted	4	31	42

*Data from 1971, a peak year for draft offenses, *Statistical Abstract of the United States*, 1973.

**The base figures were derived from the number of draft cases referred to the Justice Department, and the number of violent and property offenses cleared and reported to the FBI.

TABLE 17

NUMBER OF DRAFT-AGE AMERICAN MALE IMMIGRANTS TO CANADA
BY AGE AND YEAR

Year	15–19	20–24	25–29
1964	298	412	663
1965	310	696	916
1966	478	910	1,059
1967	581	1,233	1,218
1968	620	1,999	1,457
1969	646	2,175	1,584
1970	657	2,929	1,924
1971	667	2,135	1,976
1972	583	1,522	1,875
1973	661	1,488	1,971
1974	656	1,369	2,230
Totals (1965–1972)	4,542	13,599	12,009

Note: In addition to the statistics presented above, 1,200 draft-age American males became landed immigrants during Canada's 1972 amnesty for illegal immigrants.

Sources: Annual Canadian Immigration Statistics with help from the staff at the Canadian embassy.

135

TABLE 18

ESTIMATES OF AMERICANS WHO TOOK EXILE IN CANADA
BETWEEN 1965 AND 1972

| | ASSUMPTIONS | | | ESTIMATES* | | |
Age	Assumption 1	Assumption 2	Assumption 3	Low estimate	Mean	High estimate
19	706	2,158	2,814	706	1,432	2,158
20–24	5,859	10,303	13,599	10,303	11,951	13,599
25	1,473	6,605	7,769	6,605	4,621	7,769
Total:	8,038	19,066	24,182	17,614	18,004	23,556
					+ 1,200**	
			Legal Immigrants:		19,204	
			Illegal Immigrants:		10,000***	
			Estimated Total:		30,000	

Assumption 1:   Nondraft/AWOL-motivated immigration to Canada increased in a straight-line manner between 1964 and 1973. This assumes that no immigration in 1964 or 1973 was draft/AWOL motivated and that draft/AWOL motivated immigration can be measured by subtracting a constantly rising baseline from the annual immigration totals for 1965 through 1972.

Assumption 2:   Nondraft/AWOL-motivated immigration to Canada remained constant from 1964 through 1972. This assumes that no immigration in 1964 was draft/AWOL-motivated and that draft/AWOL-motivated immigration can be measured by subtracting a constant baseline from the annual immigration totals for 1965 through 1972.

Assumption 3:   This assumes that all immigration of nineteen to twenty-five year-olds was draft/AWOL-motivated between 1965 and 1972, and that draft/AWOL-motivated immigration can be calculated by subtracting a constant baseline of fifteen to eighteen and twenty-six to twenty-nine year-olds (taken from the 1964 data) from the annual immigration totals for 1965 through 1972.

---

*High and low estimates are derived from apparent trends in the data.
**1,200 illegal immigrants obtained landed immigrant status through a special Canadian policy in 1972, a fact nont reflected in the above statistics.
***Canadian immigration counselors believed that there was approximately one illegal immigrant for every two legal immigrants during the Vietnam era not counting those who came to Canada for just a few days.

TABLE 19

AMERICAN EXPATRIATES IN CANADA

Year	Number of American males obtaining citizenship	Approximate number of Vietnam-induced expatriates*
1964–67	not applicable	0
1968	730	0
1969	731	1
1970	787	57
1971	960	230
1972	1,233	503
1973	1,781	1,051
1974	2,529	1,799
1975	not available	?
1976	not available	?
	Total:	3,631
	Estimate for 1975–76:	1,400
	Total 1969–76:	5,000

*These figures are derived by subtracting the 1968 base tally of 730 from subsequent tallies. Because of Canada's five-year waiting period, the first draft-motivated exiles who became Canadian citizens were not eligible for citizenship before 1969.

Source: Annual Canadian Citizenship Statistics.

TABLE 20

PRESIDENTIAL CLEMENCY PROGRAM
APPLICATION TOTALS

Agency	Applicants	Number eligible	Number applying	Percent applying
Defense	Fugitive AWOL offenders	10,115	5,615	56
Justice	Unconvicted draft offenders	4,522	736	17
PCB	Discharged AWOL offenders	90,000	13,589	15
PCB	Convicted draft offenders	8,700	1,879	22
	TOTAL:	113,337	21,819	20

COMPARISON OF DISPOSITIONS FOR DIFFERENT PHASES
OF PRESIDENTIAL CLEMENCY PROGRAM
(in percentages)

	PCB* Civilian	PCB** Military	Justice	Defense
0 months alternative service***	81.5	36.2	0	1.1
1-3 months alternative service	8.0	20.0	1.0	0.8
4-6 months alternative service	5.2	23.1	4.7	3.1
7-9 months alternative service	1.4	10.2	2.3	4.5
10-12 months alternative service	2.0	3.5	6.5	6.9
13 + months alternative service	0.5	0.2	85.5	83.6
No clemency	1.5	6.9	0	0

*Clemency Board phase for convicted draft offenders.
**Clemency Board phase for convicted military offenders.
***Months of alternative service.

Source: Presidential Clemency Board *Report,* p. 123.

TABLE 21
FORD CLEMENCY PROGRAM

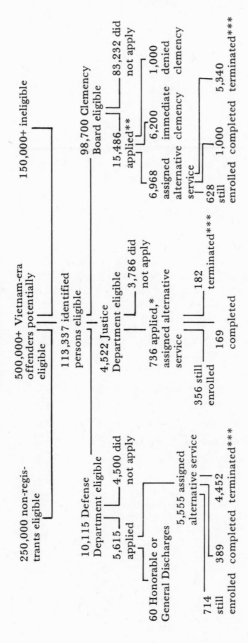

250,000 non-regis-
trants eligible

500,000+ Vietnam-era
offenders potentially
eligible

150,000+ ineligible

113,337 identified
persons eligible

98,700 Clemency
Board eligible

15,486
applied**

83,232 did
not apply

6,200
immediate
clemency

1,000
denied
clemency

6,968
assigned
alternative
service

628
still
enrolled

1,000
completed

5,340
terminated***

10,115 Defense
Department eligible

4,522 Justice
Department eligible

3,786 did
not apply

736 applied,*
assigned alternative
service

356 still
enrolled

169
completed

182
terminated***

5,615
applied

4,500 did
not apply

5,555 assigned
alternative service

714
still
enrolled

389
completed

4,452
terminated***

60 Honorable or
General Discharges

Alternative Service figures as of October 27, 1976.

* 31 applicants had their indictments dismissed.
** Approximately 700 of these cases await Presidential action, and 180 are undecided.
*** This includes those who never contacted Selective Service.

SOURCE NOTES

Vietnam Generation

Basic generational data comes from the *Statistical Abstract of the United States* and from the Defense Department's *Military Manpower Statistics*. The number of Vietnam veterans in the generation (2,150,000) is smaller than the total number of Vietnam veterans (2,500,000) because of the involvement of servicemen of nondraft-eligible age.

Civilian Offenders

Data on nonregistrants, draft-avoidance, and unreported draft offenders are from the Vietnam Generation Survey, conducted specially for the Vietnam Offender Study. Statistics about the number of reported draft offenders are official Justice Department data. Information on draft case dismissals are based on interviews with federal prosecutors in 15 districts. Indictment, trial, and conviction data on draft violations are from the *Annual Reports* of the Administrative Office of the U.S. Courts. Punishment data are from the Clemency Board's *Report to the President*. Characteristics of draft offenders are based on the Clemency Board's survey of 472 civilian applicants. Statistics about draft card offenses come from public statements made by Justice Department officials, and the number of Vietnam related tax offenses comes from *Peacemaker* magazine.

Ford Clemency Program

Background data on the Ford clemency program comes from
the Clemency Board's *Report to the President,* the Defense Department's *After Action Report,* and monthly alternative service
reports of the Selective Service System. Additional data come
from interviews with military personnel and civilian counselors
at Fort Harrison (the Joint Clemency Processing Center) and
Fort Dix. The number of inactive Justice Department cases
prior to the Kennedy list is derived from a survey by the Public
Law Institute of 3,362 individuals who made inquiry concerning
their draft violation liability. Alternative service projections are
derived through interviews of twelve Selective Service state direc-
tors. Budget estimates come from interviews of federal officials
connected with the various phases of the clemency program.

Exiles and Expatriates

Official Canadian immigration and naturalization statistics
have been used to estimate the extent of American migration to
that country. The assumptions underlying the 30,000 figure are
explained in exile tables in the appendix. Swedish figures are based
on official tallies conducted by that government. The 10,000 estimate of non-Canadian exiles is based upon the ratio of Canadian
versus non-Canadian fugitives of the Ford program. Clemency
program statistics suggest that the number of military exiles
was about 15,000, from which the draft exile population of
25,000 can be derived. The 5,000 expatriate estimate is based
on official Canadian citizenship statistics for 1968 through 1974.

The Recommended Program of Relief

Eligibility figures are based on estimates and tallies described
in other source notes. Case-by-case projections are based on
Clemency Board survey data. Veterans' benefits eligibility projections are based on Clemency Board and Defense Department
(MARDAC) data.

Military Offenders

Basic statistics about military manpower and discharges are
provided by the Defense Department's *Selected Manpower Sta-*

tistics (May 1975). Data about the characteristics of discharged soldiers was furnished by the Defense Department's MARDAC division for the 1975 House Hearings on Administrative Discharges. Data about bad discharges and the circumstances of absence offenses are provided by the Clemency Board's survey of 1,009 military participants in its program and supplemented by information obtained from U.S. Army Judiciary and the U.S. Navy Judiciary. Data about the characteristics of individual absentees comes primarily from the Clemency Board survey, *The Vietnam Era Deserter* (a July 1976 study by Army Research Institute for the Behavioral and Social Sciences), and Hamilton I. McCubbin's *Situational and Leadership Factors Related to AWOL* (July 1971). Data about marginally qualified soldiers come from the Clemency Board survey, the MARDAC statistics, and the Defense Department's analysis of Project 100,000. Statistics measuring the impact of bad discharges on civilian employment opportunities are extracted from Bradley Jones's 1973 study in the *Military Law Review* (Volume 53) and William Pearman's "Analysis of the Impact of Clemency Discharges," published in the Clemency Board's *Report to the President.*

SELECTED BIBLIOGRAPHY

The Vietnam-Era Draft

Canby, Steven L. *Military Manpower Procurement* (a Rand Corporation Study). Lexington, Massachusetts: Lexington Books, 1972.

Davis, James W., and Dolbeare, Kenneth M. *Little Groups of Neighbors: The Selective Service System* Chicago: Markham Publishing, 1968.

Fallows, James "Vietnam—the Class War." *The National Observer*, February 21, 1976.

Gerhardt, Roger W., ed. *The Draft and Public Policy.* Columbus, Ohio: Ohio State University Press, 1971.

In Pursuit of Equity: Who Serves When Not All Serve? (report of the National Advisory Commission on Selective Service, February 1967).

Little, Roger W., ed. *Selective Service and American Society.* New York: Russell Sage Foundation, 1969.

O'Sullivan, John, and Meckler, Alan M., eds. *The Draft and its Enemies: A Documentary History*. Urbana, Illinois, University of Illinois Press, 1974.

Tatum, Arlo, and Tuchinsky, Joseph. *Guide to the Draft.* Boston: Beacon Press, 1969.

U.S., Congress, House, Armed Services Committee, Special Subcommittee on the Draft, *Hearings on Review of the Administration and Operation of the Draft Law*, 91st Cong., 2d sess., July, 1970.

U.S., Congress, Senate, Armed Services Committee, *Hearings on Amending and Extending the Draft Laws*, 90th Cong., 1st sess., April, 1967.

U.S. Congress, Senate, Judiciary Committee, Subcommittee on Administrative Practice and Procedures, *Hearings on the Selective Service: Its Operation, Practices, and Procedures*, 91st Cong., 1st sess., October-November, 1969.

U.S., Department of Defense, Defense Manpower Commission, *Defense Manpower: The Keystone of National Security*, a report to the president and the Congress, April 1976.

Vietnam Generation Survey of 1,586 young men in Washington, D.C., South Bend, Indiana, and Ann Arbor, Michigan, who were of draft age during the Vietnam war. This survey was conducted by the Vietnam Offender Study.

Willenz, June A., ed. *Dialogue on the Draft* (report of the National Conference on the Draft). Washington, D.C.: American Veterans Committee, 1966.

Civilian Offenders

Clemency Board Survey of 472 convicted draft offenders.

Ferber, Michael, and Lynd, Staughton. *The Resistance*. Boston, Massachusetts: Beacon Press, 1971.

Gaylin, Willard. *In the Service of Their Country*. New York: Grossett and Dunlop, 1970.

Gutknecht, David, et al.. *Check Out the Odds*. Minneapolis, Minnesota: Twin Cities Resistance, 1971.

Lynd, Alice. *We Won't Go*. Boston: Beacon Press, 1968.

Peacemaker Magazine

Useem, Michael. *Conscription, Protest, and Social Conflict: The Life and Death of a Draft Resistance Movement*. New York: John C. Wiley and Sons, 1973.

U.S., Department of Commerce *Statistical Abstract of the United States*. 1973.

U.S., Congress, Senate, Judiciary Committee, Subcommittee on Administrative Practice and Procedures, *Hearings on Selective Service and Amnesty*, 92d Cong., 2d sess., February-March, 1972.

Enforcement of the Draft Laws

Draft Counselor's Newsletter. San Francisco, California: CCCO.
"Sentencing Selective Service Violators: A Judicial Wheel of
      Fortune," *Columbia Law Journal* 5. no. 2 (August 1969).
Selective Service Law Reporter.
U.S., Congress House, Armed Services Committee, Subcommittee
      on the Draft, *Hearings to Amend Military Selective Service
      Act of 1967,* 91st Cong., 1st sess., September, 1969.
U.S., Congress, House, Armed Services Committee, Subcommittee
      on the Volunteer Armed Force and Selective Service, *Hearings
      on Volunteer Forces and Selective Service,* 92d Cong., 2d sess.,
      March, 1972.
U.S., Department of Justice, *Federal Offenders in United States
      District Courts,* Administrative Office of the United States
      Courts, Annual Selective Service violation statistics.
U.S., Selective Service System, *Legal Aspects of Selective Service,*
      January 1, 1973.
U.S., Selective Service System, *Semi-Annual Reports of the Direc-
      tor of Selective Service,* 1965-1975.

The Vietnam-Era Military

Ambrose, Stephen E., and Barber, James A., Jr., eds. *The Military
      and American Society.* New York: Free Press, 1972.
Bachman, Jerald G., and Blair, John D. *Soldiers, Sailors, and Ci-
      vilians: The Military Mind and the All-Volunteer Force.* The
      University of Michigan, Institute of Social Research, 1975.
Binkin, Martin, and Johnston, John. *All Volunteer Armed Forces:
      Progress, Problems, and Prospects,* Report prepared for the
      Senate Armed Services Committee, June 1, 1973.
Cortright, David. *Soldiers in Revolt: The American Military Today.*
      New York: Doubleday, 1975.
Glick, Edward B. *Soldiers, Scholars and Society: The Social Impact
      of the American Military.* Pacific Palisades, California: Good-
      year Publishing, 1971.
Helmer, John. *Bringing the War Home: The American Soldier Before
      Vietnam and After,* The Free Press: New York, 1974.
Johnson, Hayes, and Wilson, George. *Army in Anguish.* New York:
      Pocket Books, 1971.

Loory, Stuart H. *Defeated: Inside America's Military Machine.* New York: Random House, 1973.

Moskos, Charles C. *The American Enlisted Man: The Rank and File in Today's Military.* New York: Russell Sage Foundation, 1970.

Starr, Paul. *The Discarded Army: Veterans After Vietnam.* New York: Charterhouse, 1973.

U.S., Department of the Army, Personnel Office. *Analysis of Casualties by Learning Abilities,* June 28, 1968.

U.S., Department of Defense, Office of the Comptroller. *Selected Manpower Statistics.*

Military Offenders

Bell, D. Bruce, and Houston, Thomas J. *The Vietnam Era Deserter: Characteristics of Unconvicted Army Deserters Participating in the Presidential Clemency Program.* U.S. Army Research Institute for the Behavioral and Social Sciences, July, 1976.

Clemency Board Survey of 1,009 Convicted Military Fugitives.

McCubbin, Hamilton I., et. al. *Leadership and Situational Factors Related to AWOL: A Research Report.* Fort Riley, Texas: U.S. Army Correctional Training Facility, 1971.

U.S., Congress, House, Appropriations Committee, Subcommittee, *Hearings on Department of Defense Appropriations for 1972, Morale and Discipline in the Army,* 92d Cong., 2d sess., 1972.

U.S., Congress, Senate, Armed Services Committee, *Hearings on Military Deserters,* 90th Cong., 2 sess., May, 1968.

U.S., Congress, Senate, Armed Services Committee, Subcommittee on Drug Abuse in the Military, *Hearings on Drug Abuse in the Military,* 92d Cong., 2d sess., February, 1972.

Military Discipline

Addlestone, David F., and Hewman, Susan H. *ACLU Practice Manual on Military Discharge Upgrading.* Military Rights Project of the ACLU Project on Amnesty, 1975.

Effron, Andrew. "Punishment of Enlisted Personnel Outside the

UCMJ: A Statutory and Equal Protection Analysis of Military Discharge Policies." *Harvard Civil Liberties Law Review* 9, no. 2 (March 1974).

Jones, Bradley. "The Gravity of Administrative Discharges: A Legal and Empirical Evaluation." *Military Law Review* 59 (Winter 1973).

Military Law Reporter.

U.S., Congress, House, Armed Services Committee, *Hearings on Administrative Discharges* (unpublished), 94th Cong., 1st sess., November, 1975.

U.S., Congress, House, Armed Services Committee, *Hearings on H.R. 523, Administrative Discharges,* 92d Cong., 1st sess., June-July, 1971.

Exiles and Expatriates

Amex Canada.

Annual Canadian Citizenship Statistics.

Annual Canadian Immigration Statistics.

Emerick, Kenneth. *War Resisters, Canada.* Knox, Pa.: Knox Free Press, 1972.

Franks, Lucinda. *Waiting Out a War.* New York: Coward, McCann, and Geoghegan, 1974.

Hayes, Thomas Lee. *American Deserters in Sweden.* New York: Associated Press, 1971.

Jones, Douglas, and Raish, David. "American Deserters and Draft Evaders: Exile, Punishment, or Amnesty." *Harvard International Law Journal* 3, no. 1 (Winter 1972).

Killmer, Richard, et. al., *They Can't Go Home Again.* Philadelphia: United Church Press, 1971.

Whitmore, Terry. *Memphis-Nam-Sweden.* New York: Doubleday, 1971.

Williams, Roger Neville. *The New Exiles: American War Resisters in Canada.* New York: Liveright Publishers, 1971.

Presidential Clemency Program

Bell, D. Bruce, and Houston, Thomas J. *The Vietnam Era Deserter:*

Characteristics of Unconvicted Army Deserters Participating in the Presidential Clemency Program. U.S. Army Research Institute for the Behavioral and Social Sciences, July, 1976.

Pearman, William A. "An Analysis of the Impact of Clemency Discharges on Recipients' Employment Opportunities." In *Report to the President,* Presidential Clemency Board. p. 403.

Report to the Service Secretaries by the Joint Alternative Service Board in Support of Presidential Proclamation 4313.

U.S., Congress, House, Judiciary Committee, Subcommittee on Courts, Civil Liberties, and the Administration of Justice, *Hearings on Amnesty,* 93d Cong., 2d sess., March, 1974.

U.S., Congress, House, Judiciary Committee, Subcommittee on Courts, Civil Liberties, and the Administration of Justice, *Report on the Presidential Clemency Program,* 94th Cong., 1st sess., August, 1975.

U.S., Congress, Senate, Judiciary Committee, Subcommittee on Administrative Practice and Procedure, *Hearings on Clemency Program Practices and Procedures,* 93d Cong., 2d sess., December, 1974.

U.S., Presidential Clemency Board, *Report to the President,* 1975.

U.S., Department of Defense, Office of the Deputy Chief of Staff for Personnel, Department of the Army, *After Action Report,* report on implementation of president's clemency program, 2 vols., October 1975.

Legal Citations

Brown v. *Walker,* 161 U.S. 591 (1896).
Toussie v. *United States,* 397 U.S. 112 (1970).
United States v. *O'Brien,* 391 U.S. 367 (1968).
United States v. *Richardson,* 514 F. 2d 105 (3d Cir. 1975).